AMITIES

letter-writing practice

ENA FOWLER

Nelson

Thomas Nelson and Sons Ltd
Nelson House Mayfield Road
Walton-on-Thames Surrey
KT12 5PL UK

Nelson Blackie
Wester Cleddens Road
Bishopbriggs
Glasgow G64 2NZ UK

Thomas Nelson Australia
102 Dodds Street
South Melbourne
Victoria 3205 Australia

Nelson Canada
1120 Birchmount Road
Scarborough Ontario
M1K 5G4 Canada

© Ena Fowler 1980

I(T)P Thomas Nelson is an International
       Thomson Publishing Company

I(T)P is used under licence

First published by Harrap Limited 1980
ISBN 0-245-53544-6
Eighth impression published by
Thomas Nelson and Sons Ltd 1985
ISBN 0-17-444336-6
Second edition published by
Thomas Nelson and Sons Ltd 1989
ISBN 0-17-439205-2
NPN 9 8 7

By the same author:
La belle histoire!
Quelques mots

Acknowledgements
Our thanks are due to the following for permission
to reproduce their photographs:
Cabinet Jacques Pintureau
Commissariat Général au Tourisme
Documentation Française
Sue Chapple

Our thanks are also due to the following
Examinations Boards for permission to reproduce
the letter-writing questions from their past
examination papers:
London East Anglian Group
Midland Examining Group
Northern Examining Association
Scottish Examination Board
Southern Examining Group
Welsh Joint Education Committee
Northern Ireland Schools Examinations Council

Illustrated by David Farris and Caroline Ewen
Cover Illustration: Andrea Norton

Designed by SGS Associates (Education) Ltd.

Printed in China

Introduction

Amitiés is designed to prepare students for the letter-writing component of GCSE. However, examinations are by no means the only justification for this book. Any writing in French that the majority of students will do after leaving school is most likely to be in the form of a letter, whether of the informal type to a French correspondent or of a more formal nature to a **Syndicat d'Initiative** for information or to a hotel for accommodation.

The book offers a variety of letter-writing exercises including letters to a pen-friend, notes on holiday postcards, letters which invite, accept, apologize and thank, formal letters requesting information and letters to answer.

Help is given in the form of vocabulary and structure guides which, along with suggestions in English, indicate possible ways in which the model letters may be adapted, while comprehension of these model letters is assessed by a number of context questions in English. Specific practice is given in replying to letters, and in particular in identifying points that need to be answered, as this is by no means always a simple task: some questions appear very obvious, but others can be much less clearly identifiable.

It is hoped that as a result of working through this book students will gain confidence in their own ability to compose, comprehend and respond to the type of letters they are likely to have to deal with, be it in an exam or in everyday life.

Contents

Section 1
Writing about yourself

1. Yourself and your family

J'ai I have **Il a** He has **Elle a** She has	**les cheveux** hair	**noirs** black/dark **bruns** brown	**blonds** fair/blond **châtains** light brown	**roux** red **gris** grey			
	les yeux eyes	**bleus** blue **verts** green **marron** brown **noirs** black/dark **noisette** hazel **gris** grey					
	quinze 15 **quarante** 40 **quatre-vingts** 80	**ans** years					

Je suis I am **Il est** He is **Elle est** She is	**assez** quite **très** very	**petit(e)** small **grand(e)** tall **mince** slim **maigre** thin **gros(se)** fat **joli(e)** pretty **beau(belle)** attractive **laid(e)** ugly

Je m'appelle My name is **Il s'appelle** His name is **Elle s'appelle** Her name is	**John** **Sarah**

J'habite à I live in **Nous habitons à** We live in	**Londres** **Manchester**

Ma mère My mother **Mon père** My father **Ma sœur** My sister **Mon frère** My brother	**est** is	**ingénieur** engineer **professeur** teacher **instituteur (trice)** primary teacher **mineur** miner **routier** long-distance lorry driver **médecin** doctor **épicier(ière)** grocer **employé(e) de banque** bank clerk **en chômage** out of work **ménagère** housewife **infirmière** nurse **secrétaire** secretary **vendeur(euse)** shop assistant
	travaille works	**à la maison** at home **dans une usine** in a factory **dans un bureau** in an office **dans un magasin** in a shop **dans un supermarché** in a supermarket **dans un garage** in a garage **dans un hôpital** in a hospital **dans une école** in a school

Some questions to ask

Quel âge	*as-tu?* *avez-vous?*	How old are you?
As-tu *Avez-vous*	**des frères ou des sœurs?**	Have you any brothers or sisters?
Comment s'appellent-*ils/elles***?**		What are their names?
Comment sont-*ils/elles***?**		What are they like?
Que font	*tes* *vos*	**parents dans la vie?**	What do your parents do?

Exercise 1

    a)   Give the name and age of everyone in your family.
    b)   Describe 5 young people you know. Say how old they are. Give the colour of their hair and eyes. Say whether they are tall or small, fat or thin.
    c)   Describe five adults. Say where they live and what their work is.

Exercise 2

Read the following letter, and answer in English the questions which follow:

> Versailles, le 1ᵉʳ Septembre
>
> Chère Julie,
>
> Mon professeur de français m'a donné ton adresse. Je suis très content d'avoir une correspondante anglaise. J'ai seize ans, et mon anniversaire est le premier juin. J'ai un frère, plus âgé que moi (il a dix-sept ans), et une sœur qui a dix ans seulement. J'ai les yeux bruns et les cheveux bruns. Mon frère me ressemble, mais ma sœur a les yeux bleus, ce qui est assez rare en France. Je suis grand et maigre, ainsi que mon frère, mais ma sœur, qui s'appelle Anne-Marie, est petite. Ma mère est petite et jolie, mais je dois dire que mon père est assez gros.
>
>   Mon père est ingénieur, et ma mère est secrétaire. Nous habitons à Versailles, pas très loin de Paris. C'est une ville fort intéressante (le fameux château de Louis Quatorze se trouve à Versailles) mais j'habite assez loin de l'école, ce qui n'est pas très commode.
>
>   J'espère recevoir de tes nouvelles bientôt – et une photo!
>   Ton nouvel ami,
>   Robert.

1.   How old is Robert, and when is his birthday?
2.   Describe his brother – his age and appearance.
3.   Describe his sister.
4.   What work do his parents do?
5.   What does Robert say about Versailles?

Exercise 3

Copy out the following letter, filling in the gaps:

ADDRESS

DATE

Cher Robert,
Je te remercie de ta gentille lettre. Moi aussi, je suis
très content(e) d'avoir un correspondant. J'ai............ans, et mon anniversaire est............ . J'ai un frère; il s'appelle............et il a............ans. Il a
les cheveux............et les yeux............et il est............ .
J'ai deux sœurs. L'une s'appelle............et elle a............ans.
Elle a les cheveux............et les yeux............, et elle est............ . L'autre, qui
a............ans, s'appelle............ . Elle a les cheveux............ et les yeux............ .
Mon père travaille............ et ma mère est............ . Nous habitons à
.... C'est une ville............ mais pas très............
Écris-moi bientôt.

Ton/Ta nouvel(le) ami(e),

NAME

Excercise 4

Write a first letter to your own French correspondent, along the following lines:

Thanks for his/her letter. Names and description of your family. Points about them you particularly like or dislike, or find interesting. A brief description of the town where you live.

2. Your friends and your interests

Je préfère I prefer **J'aime beaucoup** I very much like **Je n'aime pas** I don't like **Il/Elle aime** He/She likes	**jouer au football** to play football **jouer au rugby** to play rugby **jouer au volleyball** to play volleyball **jouer au netball** to play netball **jouer au ping-pong** to play table-tennis **jouer au baby-foot** to play table-football **jouer au tennis** to play tennis **jouer de la guitare** to play the guitar **jouer du piano** to play the piano **jouer du violon** to play the violin **écouter des disques** to listen to records **regarder la télévision** to watch the television **regarder les matchs de football** to watch football matches **sortir avec des amis** to go out with friends **bavarder avec des amis** to chat with friends **aller au Club des Jeunes** to go to the Youth Club
J'ai I have **Je voudrais** I would like **Il/Elle voudrait** He/She would like	**un transistor** a transistor radio **un électrophone** a record player **un vélo** a bike **un scooter** a moped **une moto** a motor-bike
C'est It's	**agréable** pleasant **amusant** amusing **passionnant** exciting **ennuyeux** boring

Some questions to ask

Aimes-tu Do you like	**jouer au football?** **jouer de la guitare?** **sortir avec tes amis?**	playing football? playing the guitar? going out with your friends?
Quand est-ce que When **Avec qui est-ce que** With whom	**tu sors?** **tu joues?**	do you go out? do you play?
Qu'est-ce que What	**tu aimes faire?**	do you like doing?
Que fais-tu What do you do	**le soir?** **le weekend?** **le samedi?**	in the evenings? at the weekends? on Saturdays?

Exercise 1

    a)   Name three pastimes which you enjoy, and three which you do not enjoy.

    b)   Describe a friend's interests in the same way.

    c)   Complete: J'ai un..........., un........... et un..........., mais je n'ai pas de........... . Je voudrais un........... .

Exercise 2

Read the following letter, and answer in English the questions which follow:

3, Hanks Road
London, N.W.3.
le 10 septembre

Cher Robert,

J'ai été très contente de recevoir ta lettre — merci bien. Je suis de retour à l'école déjà, tandis que toi, tu es toujours en vacances — tu as de la chance! Mais ce n'est pas trop mal, car j'ai deux amies, et nous nous amusons bien ensemble. Ma meilleure amie s'appelle Susie. Elle a quinze ans. Elle est petite et jolie. Elle a les cheveux blonds. L'autre s'appelle Debbie. Elle est plus grande que Susie. Elle a les yeux bruns et les cheveux noirs.

Que fais-tu le soir? Moi, je n'aime pas faire mes devoirs! C'est trop ennuyeux. Quand j'ai fini mes devoirs, le soir, je vais souvent chez Susie qui habite tout près, et nous écoutons ses disques. Susie aime jouer de la guitare aussi. Debbie aime regarder la télévision, et le mardi, elle vient chez moi voir un programme que nous aimons beaucoup. Nous entendons tous les disques les plus populaires de la semaine, et quelquefois nous voyons nos chanteurs favoris. Quels chanteurs préfères-tu? Et quelles sortes de programmes de télévision aimes-tu regarder?

Le samedi, nous aimons aller au Club des Jeunes. Là, nous dansons, ou écoutons des disques. On peut aussi jouer au ping-pong.

Et toi, vas-tu au Club des Jeunes? As-tu un électrophone? J'en ai un. J'ai un vélo aussi, mais je voudrais un scooter.

Écris-moi bientôt.

Amitiés,

Julie.

1. Why is Robert lucky, and Julie unlucky?
2. Describe Susie and Debbie.
3. What are Susie's interests?
4. What are Debbie's interests?
5. When do they go to the Youth Club? What do they do there?
6. What five questions does Julie ask Robert?

Exercise 3

Write a letter of your own to Robert, describing your friends. What do they look like? What are their favourite pastimes, and yours? How do you spend the evenings during the week and at week-ends?

3. Your home

		au rez-de-chaussée on the ground floor **au premier étage** on the first floor **au sixième étage** on the sixth floor	**d'un immeuble** of a block of flats **d'un H.L.M.** of a fixed-rent block of flats (like council flats)
Mon appartement My flat	**est** is		
Ma maison My house		**grand(e)** large **petit(e)** small **en brique** made of brick **en pierre** made of stone	

	au centre de la ville in the centre of town **dans la banlieue** in the suburbs **à la campagne** in the country **dans un village** in a village **loin de la ville** a long way from town **près de la ville** near the town
Il/Elle se trouve It is situated	

		six pièces six rooms **trois chambres** three bedrooms **une salle à manger** a dining-room **un salon** a sitting-room **une cuisine** a kitchen **une salle de bains** a bathroom **un cabinet de toilette** a toilet **un jeu de billard** a billiard table
En tout In all **Au rez-de-chaussée** On the ground floor **En haut** Upstairs **Dans le grenier** In the attic **Au sous-sol** In the cellar	**il y a** there is/ there are	

Exercise 1

Imagine you are an estate-agent. Make up advertisements to sell the following houses and flats:

a) A flat on the 2nd floor of a block of flats in the centre of town: kitchen, large living-room, three bedrooms, bathroom; parking space.

b) Large stone-built house, in the centre of town, cellar, attic and six rooms: sitting-room, dining-room, kitchen, two bedrooms, bathroom; garage.

c) Small stone-built house, in a village, four rooms in all: sitting-room, kitchen, one bedroom, bathroom; no garage.

Exercise 2

Read the following letter, and answer in English the questions which follow:

Versailles, le 17 septembre

Chère Julie,

Merci bien pour ta lettre, que j'ai reçue lundi. Je te remercie de ta photo aussi. Je l'ai montrée à mon copain Simon. Il a dit que tu es très jolie, et alors, lui aussi, il veut une correspondante anglaise!

Tu me demandes de décrire ma maison. J'habite aux environs de Versailles. Ma maison est petite et en brique. En tout, il y a sept pièces. Au rez-de-chaussée il y a une salle à manger, un salon et une cuisine. Dans le salon il y a un téléviseur, des fauteuils et un sofa.

En haut il y a trois chambres et une salle de bains. Mes parents couchent dans la plus grande chambre, ma sœur dans la plus petite, et mon frère Henri et moi partageons la troisième chambre.

Au grenier, nous avons installé une discothèque. Nous avons peint les murs en blanc et rouge, et nous y avons mis les photos de nos chanteurs favoris. Moi, je joue de la guitare, et mon copain Jules aime jouer de la batterie. Nous nous y amusons beaucoup tous les samedis.

Samedi dernier, nous faisions tant de bruit que notre voisin M. Hulot a téléphoné et a crié, "Ne savez-vous pas qu'il est minuit? Je ne peux pas dormir avec ce bruit affreux!" Il a soixante ans, donc il ne sait pas estimer la valeur de nos chansons, évidemment! Nous avons dû nous excuser, et j'ai fait du jardinage pour lui dimanche.

Écris-moi bientôt, et fais la description de ta maison.

Amitiés,

Robert.

1. What did Simon say about Julie's photo, and what was the result?
2. Where does Robert live?
3. What type of house is it?
4. Describe the rooms downstairs and upstairs.
5. Describe the attic.
6. When and why did M. Hulot telephone?
7. What did Robert do to make up for this?

Exercise 3

Write a letter to Robert or to your own correspondent, describing your house. Where is the house situated? Is it made of brick, stone, etc.? How many rooms are there? What rooms are there downstairs/upstairs? Is there a garden or a garage? Mention any other points you think will be interesting.

4. At the Youth Club

J'aime beaucoup I very much like **Nous aimons** We like **Je préfère** I prefer **Je m'amuse à** I have fun **Je passe mon temps à** I spend my time **Je n'aime pas** I don't like **Je ne sais pas** I don't know how to	**jouer au ping-pong** playing table-tennis **jouer au baby-foot** playing table-football **jouer au billard** playing billiards **jouer de la guitare** playing the guitar **bavarder avec Jean** chatting with John **boire du café** drinking coffee **écouter des disques** listening to records **danser** dancing
C'est It's	**agréable** pleasant **épatant** great

Exercise 1

John and Sarah have filled in a questionnaire about their interests. Express the results in French.

Name: John Coates			
Do you like . . . ?	A little	.A lot	Not at all
Table - tennis		✓	
Table - football		✓	
Billiards	✓		
Listening to records		✓	
Dancing			✓
Is there anything else you prefer? State here: *I prefer playing football.*			

Name: Sarah Jones			
Do you like . . . ?	A little	A lot	Not at all
Table - tennis	✓		
Table - football	✓		
Billiards			✓
Listening to records		✓	
Dancing		✓	
Is there anything else you prefer? State here: *I like playing volleyball*			

xercise 2

Read the following letter, and answer the questions which follow:

3, Hanks Rd,
London, N.W. 3.
le 24 septembre

Cher Robert,

Merci pour ton petit mot. Mon amie Susie veut bien écrire à Simon. Voici son adresse:

Miss S. Brown, 7, Hanks Road, London, N.W. 3.

J'espère que la rentrée des classes n'était pas trop ennuyeuse. Que fais-tu pour t'amuser le soir? Moi, je vais au Club des Jeunes deux fois par semaine - le vendredi et le samedi, généralement. On s'y amuse beaucoup. Moi j'aime danser, mais Susie préfère écouter les disques. La semaine dernière, il y a eu une bagarre quand des inconnus sont arrivés, un peu ivres. La police est venue et on a arrêté les intrus.

J'ai déjà dit que Susie joue de la guitare. Debbie chante assez bien (du moins, elle le croit!) et nous avons formé un groupe - les "Peaux-bleues". C'est épatant! Nous avons visité des clubs dans les villes voisines. Nous avons gagné cent francs la semaine dernière - mais c'était exceptionnel.

N'oublie pas de m'écrire,
Bien à toi,
Julie

1. When does Julie go to the Youth Club?
2. How do she and Susie like to spend the time there?
3. Why was there a fight?
4. How did it end?
5. Describe the group they have formed.

xercise 3

Copy out the following letter, filling in the gaps:

ADDRESS
DATE

her Robert,

Merci pour ton petit mot. Moi aussi, j'aime aller au Club des Jeunes. J'y vais le................ .
aime beaucoup............... et............... mais je n'aime pas................ . Mon ami(e)...............
référe............... et............... . Quelquefois nous nous amusons à................ . Si mon ami(e) n'est
as là, je passe le temps à............... .

Le surveillant est très gentil. Il s'appelle............... . Il a........... ans, et il est............... . Il a les
eux............... et les cheveux........... .

(ADD A LITTLE NEWS OF YOUR OWN)

Écris-moi bientôt.
Amitiés,
NAME.

13

5. Your Saturday job

Le samedi On Saturdays	je travaille I work	au marché at the market au supermarché at the supermarket à la caisse at the cash-desk dans un magasin in a shop dans une librairie in a bookshop dans un garage in a garage comme "baby-sitter" as a baby-sitter
Je dois I have to **J'aime** I like **Je n'aime pas** I don't like		vendre les marchandises selling the goods faire les additions doing the bills bavarder avec les clients chatting with the customers arranger les rayons tidying the shelves
Ma patronne/Mon patron est My boss is		gentil(le) nice assez aimable quite likeable affreux(euse) awful épatant(e) great!

Je gagne I earn	une livre £1 neuf francs 9F cinq livres £5 cinquante francs 50 F	par heure an hour par jour a day

Je travaille I work	6 heures par jour 6 hours a day de 9 heures jusqu'à midi from 9 till 12 et de 2 heures jusqu'à 5 heures and from 2 till 5

Avec l'argent que je gagne With the money I earn	je vais I'm going to	acheter buy	des vêtements clothes un blue-jeans jeans des maillots T-shirts, jerseys des disques records un électrophone a record-player un vélo a bike un scooter a scooter une moto a motor-bike
			aller aux discos go to discos aller au cinéma go to the cinema aller en France go to France voyager à l'étranger travel abroad faire des excursions go on day trips

Some questions to ask

As-tu Avez-vous	un emploi?	Have you a job?
Que	fais-tu? faites-vous?	What do you do?
Combien	gagnes-tu? gagnez-vous?	How much money do you earn?

Exercise 1

Read the following letter, and answer in English the questions which follow:

Versailles, le 12 octobre

Chère Julie,

Je m'excuse de ne pas avoir écrit plus tôt – c'est que j'ai été enrhumé.

J'ai de bonnes nouvelles à t'annoncer – j'ai réussi à obtenir un petit emploi le samedi, ce qui me plaît beaucoup, car je n'ai jamais assez d'argent de poche. Je vends des disques. Je m'amuse bien, car il faut jouer les disques pour les clients, et je peux écouter tous les disques qui sont "dans le vent".

Mon copain Jules travaille dans un supermarché. Il travaille pour le boucher. Il apporte toutes les carcasses de la chambre frigorifique ; puis le boucher les coupe en morceaux et Jules met les prix dessus. Ce n'est pas à mon goût, mais Jules aime beaucoup cela. Le salaire est bon.

Je vais économiser, et alors dans six mois j'espère acheter un scooter. Et toi, qu'est-ce que tu fais le samedi? Est-ce que tu gagnes de l'argent de poche, comme moi? Dis-moi ce que tu fais.

Amitiés,

Robert.

1. Why is Robert's letter late?
2. What is Robert's good news, and why is he so pleased about it?
3. What is Jules' job?
4. What is Robert's job, and what does he particularly like about it?
5. Why is Robert saving up?

Exercise 2

Write to Robert, describing your Saturday job, imaginary or real. Where do you work? What is your employer's name, and what is he or she like? Describe the people you meet. What do you enjoy, or not enjoy, about the work? How much do you earn?

Exercise 3

Write to Robert describing a job you had during the last holidays. Where did you work? What were your hours of work? What were your duties? How much money did you earn and how much did you save? What did you do with the money you saved?

6. At school – the timetable

Je vais à I go to	**un collège mixte** a mixed comprehensive (11-16) **un lycée mixte** a mixed sixth form college (16-19) **une école secondaire de jeunes filles** a girls' high school **une école libre** a private school **un lycée d'enseignement professionnel** a technical college	**qui s'appelle**… which is called…

Je suis en I am in the	**terminale** second year sixth **première** first year sixth **seconde** fifth year **troisième** fourth year **quatrième** third year **cinquième** second year **sixième** first year

J'étudie I study **J'aime** I like **Je n'aime pas** I don't like **Je préfère** I prefer	**huit matières** eight subjects **les maths** maths **l'anglais** English **le français** French **l'histoire** history **la géographie** geography **la biologie** biology **la chimie** chemistry **la physique** physics **la musique** music **l'art** art **les arts ménagers** domestic science **le travail du bois** woodwork **le travail des métaux** metalwork **les études religieuses** religious education **les sports** sports **le football** football **le tennis** tennis **la natation** swimming **le hockey** hockey **le netball** netball

J'ai…heures de devoirs I have…hours' homework	**par jour** each day **par semaine** each week

Je fais mes devoirs I do my homework	**au collège** at school **à la maison/chez moi** at home **dans la bibliothèque** in the library

Je les fais I do it	**le soir** in the evenings **avant sept heures** before seven o'clock **après sept heures** after seven o'clock **entre midi et une heure** between twelve and one o'clock **avant de regarder la télé** before watching TV

Some questions to ask

Dans quelle classe es-tu?	What class are you in?
Combien de matières étudies-tu?	How many subjects do you study?
Combien d'heures de devoirs as-tu?	How many hours' homework have you?
Quand est-ce que tu fais tes devoirs?	When do you do your homework?
Où est-ce que tu fais tes devoirs?	Where do you do your homework?
Quelles matières préfères-tu?	What subjects do you like best?
Quelles matières n'aimes-tu pas?	What subjects do you not like?

Exercise 1

Below is Julie's school timetable. Write a letter in French, as though you are Julie answering Robert's questions about the timetable.

	Lundi	Mardi	Mercredi	Jeudi	Vendredi
9.40	Anglais	Français	Maths	Biologie	Anglais
10.20	Maths	Maths	Sports	Biologie	Français
11.10	Biologie	Anglais	Anglais	Français	Géographie
11.50	Biologie	Anglais	Etudes religieuses	Géographie	Géographie
2.00	Français	Maths	Sports	Français	Arts ménagers
2.40	Géographie	Etudes religieuses	Musique	Sports	Arts ménagers
3.20	Géographie	Biologie	Anglais	Maths	Arts ménagers
Devoirs					
	Géographie (40m.)	Anglais (30m.)	Anglais (30m.)	Biologie (30m.)	Géographie (40m.)
	Biologie (40m.)	Français (30m.)	Maths (30m.)	Français (30m.)	Anglais (30m.)
		Maths (30m.)		Maths (30m.)	Français (30m.)
					Arts ménagers (60m.)

Here are Robert's questions:

1. What class are you in?
2. How many subjects do you study?
3. How many hours' homework do you have each week?
4. When do you do your homework?
5. Where do you do your homework?
6. What subjects do you like best?
7. What subjects do you dislike?
8. On what days do you have   i) geography   ii) biology   iii) maths?

Exercise 2

Read the following letter, then answer in English the questions that follow:

> 3, Hanks Road,
> London, N.W.3.
> le 25 octobre
>
> Mon cher Robert,
>
> Je te remercie de ta gentille lettre. J'espère que ton rhume est guéri.
>
> Je t'écris aujourd'hui car c'est mi-trimestre, et nous avons deux jours de congé. Je ne sors pas, car il pleut. Peut-être que Susie viendra me voir ce soir. Je suis très contente d'avoir ces deux jours de congé.
>
> Cette année j'étudie huit matières, c'est-à-dire le français, l'anglais, les maths, la géographie, l'histoire, le dessin, la biologie et les arts ménagers. J'ai deux heures de dessin par semaine, (que j'aime bien) mais j'ai cinq heures de maths (que je n'aime pas!) Et toi? Quelles sont vos matières préférées? Moi, je préfère le dessin, comme je t'ai déjà dit, la biologie et l'histoire. Nous avons huit heures de devoirs par semaine, ce qui est trop, je crois.
>
> Je préfère le dessin car le professeur m'amuse. Il est très distrait. L'autre jour il est arrivé à l'école en pantoufles! Personne ne le lui a dit, et il les a portées toute la journée. Nous étions bien amusés, mais nous n'avons pas osé le lui dire.
>
> Amitiés,
> Julie.

1. What is Julie's first wish for Robert?
2. Why is Julie writing on that particular day?
3. Why is she not going out?
4. What subjects does she like/dislike?
5. What does she say about the art teacher?

Exercise 3

Write a letter to Robert or to your French correspondent, describing your school. Include the following details: The school you go to. The sort of school it is. Which year you are in. How many subjects you study. Which subjects you like most/least. Which sports you like. If you have much homework. When and where you do your homework.

Exercise 4

Write a letter to your French correspondent, describing an amusing or exciting incident which happened at school.

7. At school – how you spend the day

Je me lève à I get up at **Je pars pour l'école à** I leave for school at	**sept heures** 7 o'clock **sept heures et quart** 7.15 **sept heures et demie** 7.30

J'y vais I go there	**à pied** on foot **à moto** by motor-bike **en auto** by car **en autobus** by bus **en vélo** by bike **par le train** by train **en métro** by tube

J'arrive à I arrive at **Les cours commencent à** Lessons begin at	**huit heures vingt** 8.20 **neuf heures moins le quart** 8.45 **neuf heures dix** 9.10

Quand j'y arrive, je When I arrive there, I	**vais à la salle de classe** go to the classroom **bavarde avec mes amis** chat with my friends

La récréation est à Break is at	**dix heures cinq** 10.05 **dix heures vingt-cinq** 10.25 **onze heures moins vingt** 10.40

Pendant la récréation, je During break, I	**mange des sandwichs/du chocolat** eat sandwiches/chocolate **sors dans la cour** go out into the playground **bois du lait/café** drink milk/coffee

J'ai…leçons dans la matinée   I have…lessons during the morning

Je déjeune à I have lunch at	**midi** midday **midi et demi** 12.30

Les cours finissent à Lessons end at	**trois heures et demie** 3.30 **quatre heures** 4 o'clock

Il faut porter un uniforme   We have to wear a uniform **Il n'y a pas d'uniforme**   There is no uniform

En hiver In winter **En été** In summer	**on porte** we wear	**un veston** a jacket **un pullover** a pullover **un chemisier** a blouse **une chemise** a shirt **un pantalon** trousers **une jupe** a skirt **une robe** a dress	**noir(e)** black **gris(e)** grey **bleu(e)** blue **blanc(he)** white **vert(e)** green

Some questions to ask

A quelle heure te lèves-tu?	What time do you get up?
A quelle heure est-ce que les cours *commencent?/finissent?*	What time do the lessons begin?/end?
Que fais-tu pendant la récréation?	What do you do during break?
Est-ce qu'il faut porter un uniforme?	Is it necessary to wear a uniform?
Qu'est-ce que tu portes?	What do you wear?

Exercise 1

Imagine that yesterday was your first day at a new school, which is very different from your present one. Write a letter describing it.

Exercise 2

Read the following letter, and answer in English the questions which follow:

Versailles, le 5 novembre

Ma chère Julie,

Merci bien pour ta lettre, qui m'a beaucoup plu. J'espère que tu t'es bien amusée pendant tes deux jours de congé.

Comme je suis maintenant en première, je n'étudie pas autant de matières que toi, et ce sont les matières que je préfère, mais ce que je n'aime pas, c'est que le collège est à vingt kilomètres de la maison, et il faut donc me lever de bonne heure. J'y vais en autobus, et je mets une demi-heure à y arriver. Mes cours commencent à neuf heures moins le quart, et chaque leçon dure une heure. Je déjeune au collège, et je rentre à quatre heures et demie.

Le professeur que je préfère, c'est le professeur d'histoire. Il a une cinquantaine d'années, et il est chauve – mais il est tellement amusant – il nous fait rire tout le temps. Celle que je n'aime pas, c'est le professeur de philosophie.

L'autre jour, en garant sa voiture elle a heurté la nouvelle voiture du directeur; il n'était pas très content. Elle doit être très intelligente quand même, car elle nous a dit qu'elle a gagné une bourse et qu'elle va passer une année en Amérique, où elle va faire des conférences. Moi, je voudrais bien aller en Amérique. Aimerais-tu voyager? Quels pays voudrais-tu visiter?

N'oublie pas de m'écrire bientôt.

Ton ami,

Robert.

20

1. Now that Robert is in the sixth form, what difference does this make to his curriculum?
2. What does Robert dislike about his school?
3. How does he travel, and how long does it take him to arrive?
4. What are his comments about the history teacher?
5. What are his comments about the philosophy teacher?
6. What unfortunate incident happened as she was parking her car?
7. Why does he think she is intelligent?
8. What two questions does he ask Julie?

Exercise 3

Write a letter to Julie or to your French correspondent, giving further details about your school life, such as: how far you live from school, how you get there, how long it takes you, who your friends at school are (describe them), when your school day starts and finishes, how long your lessons last, what sports you do, what subjects you prefer, whether you have lunch at school or at home and so on. Must you wear a uniform? If so, describe what you wear.

Exercise 4

From the following pictures, describe briefly Robert's day at school.

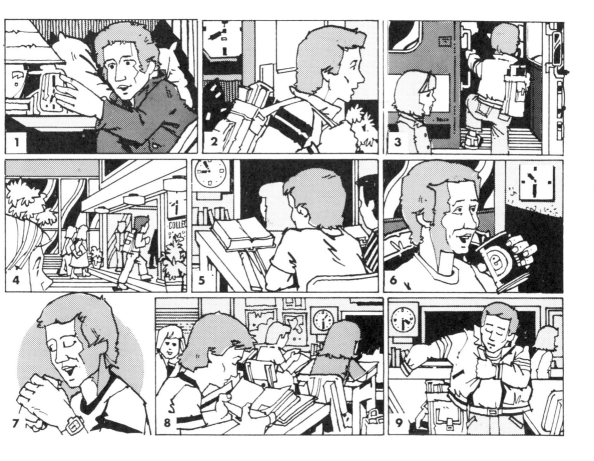

8. How you spend your evening

Je rentre *à la maison/* *chez moi* I return home	**à pied** on foot **en auto** by car **en autobus** by bus **à vélo** by bicycle **à moto** by motor-bike **par le train** by train **en métro** by tube	**à quatre heures** at 4 o'clock **à quatre heures et demie** at 4.30

Pour le goûter, je prends For tea, I have	**du gâteau** some cake **des biscuits** some biscuits **un sandwich** a sandwich **du thé** some tea **du café** some coffee

Puis je Then I	**fais mes devoirs** do my homework **promène le chien** take the dog for a walk **prépare le dîner** prepare the dinner **aide maman à préparer le dîner** help mother to prepare the dinner

Après le dîner, je After dinner, I	**fais la vaisselle** do the washing-up **sors** go out **fais mes devoirs** do my homework **lis** read **regarde la télévision** watch the TV **tricote** knit **joue au football** play football

Je me couche à I go to bed at	**dix heures** 10.00 **dix heures et demie** 10.30

Some questions to ask

A quelle heure At what time	**rentres-tu?** do you go home? **dînes-tu?** do you have dinner? **fais-tu tes devoirs?** do you do your homework? **te couches-tu?** do you go to bed?
Est-ce que tu dois Do you have to **Est-ce que tu aimes** Do you like to	**faire tes devoirs?** do your homework? **faire la vaisselle?** do the washing up? **préparer le dîner?** prepare the dinner?

Exercise 1

From the following pictures, describe Robert's evening. If you like, write as though you are Robert.

Exercise 2

Read the following letter, and answer in English the questions which follow:

> 3, Hanks Road,
> London, N.W.3.
> le 15 novembre
>
> Mon cher Robert,
> J'ai reçu ta lettre hier – merci beaucoup. Je réponds tout de suite
> parce que j'ai fini mes devoirs de bonne heure aujourd'hui, quoique d'habitude
> je n'ai pas beaucoup de temps le lundi. Généralement, je rentre de l'école à 4.30.
> Après avoir pris un sandwich et du thé, j'aide maman à préparer le dîner. Alors
> je commence mes devoirs. Après le dîner, j'aide papa à faire la vaisselle, et ensuite
> je finis mes devoirs. Puis je lis ou je tricote. Je me couche à 10.30.
>
> Et toi, qu'est-ce que tu fais le soir? Tu restes à la maison, ou tu sors?
> As-tu beaucoup de devoirs?
>
> Dans ta dernière lettre, tu me demandes si j'aimerais voyager. Ah oui,
> bien sûr. Le pays qui m'attire, c'est la Suisse – tous ces beaux lacs, et les
> jolis petits chalets. Je voudrais bien apprendre à faire du ski.
> Malheureusement, il faut aller en Écosse pour apprendre à faire du ski,
> et c'est trop loin.
> Bien à toi,
> Julie.

1. Make out an approximate timetable of Julie's evening from 4.30 onwards.
2. What does Julie ask Robert?
3. Why does she like the idea of seeing Switzerland?
4. What does she say about learning to ski in Britain?

Exercise 3

Write a letter to Julie or to your French correspondent, describing a typical evening. If you like, use the letter in Exercise 2 as a guide, replacing the underlined words with phrases of your own.

Exercise 4

Write a letter describing a) what you generally do at the weekend, or
b) what you did last weekend.

9. Describing the area where you live

C'est It is	**une grande ville importante** a large important town **une petite ville industrielle** a small industrial town **une jolie ville de province** a pretty country town			
Elle se trouve It is	**à 10 kilomètres** 10 kilometres away	**à peu près** approximately	**de** from	**Londres Birmingham Manchester**

Il y a There are	**des usines, où l'on fabrique** factories where they make	**le coton** cotton **la laine** wool **des objets en verre** glass products **des objets en plastique** plastic products

Il y a There is/ There are	**un terrain de football** a football ground **des boutiques** some small shops **de grands magasins** some big shops **un cinéma** a cinema **un jardin public** a park **une bibliothèque** a library **un théâtre** a theatre

Pour s'amuser, on peut To enjoy yourself you can	**aller aux matchs de football** go to the football matches **aller voir les magasins** go to see the shops **aller au cinéma** go to the cinema **aller au théâtre** go to the theatre **aller à la discothèque** go to the disco

Some questions to ask

Où se trouve Where is	**ton village?** **ta ville?**	your village? your town?
Est-ce qu'il y a Is there/Are there	**des usines?** **un terrain de football?** **une piscine?** **un jardin public?** **des monuments historiques?**	any factories? a football ground? a swimming baths? a park? any historic buildings?

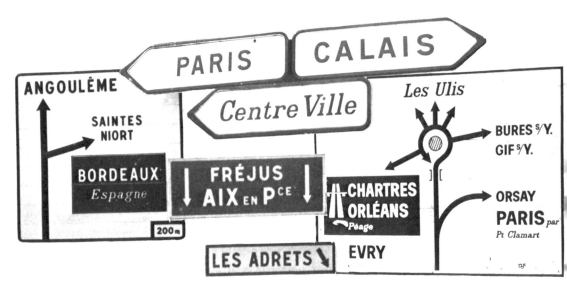

Exercise 1

Describe the town sketched below:

Exercise 2

Read the letter below, and answer in English the questions which follow:

Ma chère Julie,

Versailles, le 24 novembre

Je te remercie de ta lettre, et de la carte postale de Buckingham Palace. Nous aussi, nous avons un palais à Versailles, qui est extraordinaire. C'est Louis Quatorze qui l'a fait bâtir au dix-septième siècle. Les pièces sont très élégantes car elles sont dorées, et la chambre de la reine est aussi grande qu'un appartement entier.

Il y a une salle dont tout un mur est fait de miroirs – des centaines de miroirs! On voit aussi des tapisseries et des tableaux magnifiques.

Le palais est entouré d'un parc où se trouvent des statues et des fontaines. Je t'envoie une carte postale du "Petit Trianon", qui est construit en marbre rose. Je crois que tu aimerais bien voir ce palais.

Comment est ton arrondissement? Est-ce intéressant? Y a-t-il des monuments historiques?

N'oublie pas de m'écrire.

Ton copain,

Robert.

1. When was the palace at Versailles built?
2. Why are the rooms particularly elegant?
3. What does Robert say about the Queen's bedroom?
4. What other unusual rooms does he describe?
5. What is the particularly striking feature of the 'Petit Trianon'?

Exercise 3

Write a reply to Robert or to your French correspondent, describing your town. Include the following details. Is it large or small? Where is it? Are there any factories? What important or interesting buildings or landmarks are there? Is there a football ground? Are there any good shops? What sort of amusements are there?

Exercise 4

Write a letter describing your ideal town.

10. Your week-end

Le samedi On Saturdays **Le dimanche** On Sundays	**je me lève** I get up at	**neuf heures** 9.00 **dix heures** 10.00 **midi** 12.00

Puis, je Then, I	**me lave** wash **prends mon petit déjeuner** have my breakfast **prends un bain** have a bath **prends une douche** have a shower

Pour le petit déjeuner je prends For breakfast, I have	**du pain grillé** toast **des œufs** eggs **du bacon** bacon **du thé** tea **du café** coffee **du lait** milk

Puis, je Then, I	**fais la vaisselle** wash up **fais mon lit** make my bed **range mes affaires** tidy **lis le journal** read the paper **aide _maman/papa_** help Mum/Dad

L'après-midi, _je/j'_ In the afternoon, I	**ne fais rien** do nothing **fais des courses** go shopping **vais en ville** go into town **vais au match de football** go to the football match **nage** swim **joue au tennis** play tennis **sors avec des amis** go out with friends

Le soir, je In the evening, I	**vais danser à la discothèque** go dancing at the disco **écoute des disques** listen to records **regarde la télé** watch the TV **reste à la maison** stay at home **vais chez mon ami(e)** go to my friend's

Je me couche à I go to bed at	**onze heures** 11.00 **minuit** 12.00

Excercise 1

From the following pictures, describe Debbie's Saturday in French. If you like, write as though you are Debbie.

Exercise 2

Read the letter below, and answer in English the questions which follow:

3, Hanks Road,
London, N.W. 3.
le 5 décembre

Mon cher Robert,

Merci bien pour ta lettre, qui était très intéressante. J'écris cette lettre à la hâte car je vais sortir bientôt avec mon amie Debbie. Tous les samedis nous allons faire du lèche-vitrine, et si nous avons de l'argent, nous achetons un pull ou quelque chose comme ça.

Le soir, nous allons généralement au Club des Jeunes, mais ce soir nous allons à une surprise-partie — ça va être amusant, je crois. C'est l'anniversaire d'une amie qui s'appelle Margaret. Elle est blonde et mince et très gentille — et elle a de très bons disques. La dernière fois que nous sommes allées chez Margaret, nous avons fait tant de bruit que les voisins sont arrivés pour voir ce qui se passait — il faudra jouer les disques moins fort ce soir!

J'attends ta prochaine lettre avec impatience.

Amitiés,

Julie.

1. Why is Julie writing in a hurry?
2. What does she usually do on Saturdays?
3. What is going to happen this Saturday evening?
4. What does Julie say about Margaret?
5. What happened last time she went to Margaret's house?

Exercise 3

Write a reply to Julie, describing your Saturday or Sunday. When do you get up? What do you do in the morning? And in the afternoon? Whom do you meet? Where do you go? What do you do in the evening? When do you go to bed?

Exercise 4

Describe an interesting event which happened one week-end.

Section 2

Writing short notes and describing photos

1. A New Year's Card

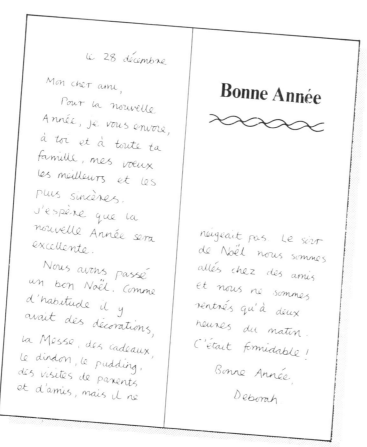

le 28 décembre

Mon cher ami,
    Pour la nouvelle
Année, je vous envoie,
à toi et à toute ta
famille, mes vœux
les meilleurs et les
plus sincères.
J'espère que la
nouvelle Année sera
excellente.
    Nous avons passé
un bon Noël. Comme
d'habitude il y
avait des décorations,
la Messe, des cadeaux,
le dindon, le pudding,
des visites de parents
et d'amis, mais il ne

Bonne Année

neigeait pas. Le soir
de Noël nous sommes
allés chez des amis
et nous ne sommes
rentrés qu'à deux
heures du matin.
C'était formidable !
    Bonne Année,
        Deborah

Write a New Year's Card to your French pen-friend, sending your good wishes and including a brief account of the Christmas you have spent.

Vocabulary

un arbre de Noël	a Christmas tree	**on m'a donné**	I was given	**on a mangé**	we ate
on a bu	we drank	**du poulet**	some chicken	**des carottes (f.)**	some carrots

2. Postcard from a seaside resort

Write a postcard to your French pen-friend from an English seaside resort.

Postcard text:

le 8 août

Chère Jeannette, Nous voici en vacances à Evian-les-Bains, petite ville très chic au bord du lac Léman.

Il y a de jolies boutiques, un cinéma, et surtout la plage et le lac. Le lac est magnifique — très calme, très beau, et l'eau est très bonne.

Ici, on peut jouer au ping pong, faire de l'escrime, danser, jouer au volleyball ou tout simplement prendre des bains de soleil. Il y a aussi le Casino, bien entendu!

Amitiés,
Marie-France

Vocabulary

il fait (du) soleil it's sunny	**il fait du vent** it's windy	**il pleut** it's raining	**le sable** sand
des rochers (m.) rocks	**des crabes (m.)** crabs	**des crevettes (f.)** shrimps	
pêcher to fish	**faire une promenade en bateau** to go for a boat-trip		

3. Postcard from a mountain resort

Write a postcard to your French pen-friend from an English mountain resort.

Chère Marie, Je m'amuse beaucoup à Chamonix. Tous les jours je fais du ski. Hier je suis tombée pour la première fois. Chaque soir nous dansons à l'hôtel. Hier j'ai fait la connaissance d'un beau jeune Français qui s'appelle Simon. Il a les cheveux noirs et les yeux bleus. Il est épatant! Amicalement, Suzette

75056.000.0024

Vocabulary

cette région this area	**beau (belle)** lovely	**boisé(e)** wooded	**on voit** you can see
montagneux(se) mountainous	**partout** everywhere	**des jonquilles (f.)** daffodils	
des jacinthes des bois (f.) bluebells	**des primevères (f.)** primroses	**des sapins** fir trees	
il y a there are	**il n'y a pas de . . .** there aren't any . . .		

4. Postcard from a camp site

Write a postcard to your French pen-friend from an English camp site.

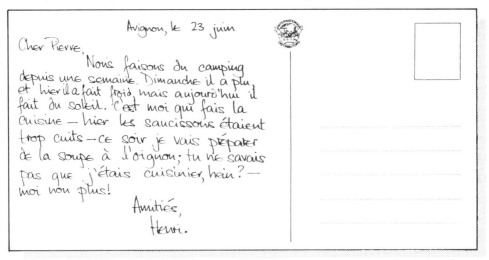

Avignon, le 23 juin

Cher Pierre,

Nous faisons du camping depuis une semaine. Dimanche il a plu, et hier il a fait froid, mais aujourd'hui il fait du soleil. C'est moi qui fais la cuisine — hier les saucissons étaient trop cuits — ce soir je vais préparer de la soupe à l'oignon; tu ne savais pas que j'étais cuisinier, hein? — moi non plus!

Amitiés,

Henri.

Vocabulary

être situé to be situated	**au bord de la mer** by the sea		**à la campagne** in the country		
dans les montagnes in the mountains	**à 6 kilomètres de** 6 km from		**la ville** the town		
le village the village	**s'amuser** to have fun	**dresser la tente** to put the tent up			
il faut + INF it is necessary	**acheter des provisions** to buy food		**demain** tomorrow		
apporter de l'eau to bring water	**un ruisseau** a stream	**hier** yesterday			

5. Describing a new friend

Write to your pen-friend, enclosing a photo of your new boy/girl friend, and describing him/her.

Il est He is **Elle est** She is	**grand(e)** tall **petit(e)** small **assez gros(se)** quite fat **mince** slim **maigre** thin **amusant** amusing **sympa(thique)** likeable				

Il a He has **Elle a** She has	**les yeux** eyes	**bruns** brown **noirs** black **gris** grey **bleus** blue
	les cheveux hair	**en brosse** crew-cut **longs** long **courts** short **plats** straight **bouclés** curly **ébouriffés** untidy

6. Describing the Family

Write a letter describing a photo of your family, which you enclose.

See also the vocabularies for 5 and 7)

Mon grand-père My grandfather			**quatre-vingts ans** 80
Ma grand-mère My grandmother			**soixante-dix ans** 70
Mon père My father			**cinquante ans** 50
Ma mère My mother	**a** is		**quarante et un ans** 41
Mon frère aîné My older brother			**dix-huit ans** 18
Mon frère cadet My younger brother			**onze ans** 11
Ma sœur aînée My older sister			**seize ans** 16
Ma sœur cadette My younger sister			**cinq ans** 5

7. Describing the class at school

Write a letter describing some of your classmates, whose photo you enclose.

Vocabulary (See also the vocabularies for 5 and 6)

au premier rang   in the first row   **au deuxième rang**   in the second row
derrière Jean   behind John   **devant Marie**   in front of Mary   **le premier**   the first (masc.)
la première   the first (fem.)   **le (la) deuxième**   the second
il/elle s'appelle   he/she is called

Section 3

Useful letters

This section deals with both formal and informal letters, and there are some differences between these which it is important to note.

Informal letters are those written between friends. The person you are writing to is normally addressed as **tu**, unless it is someone such as a pen-friend, to whom you have not written before, or someone older than yourself to whom you are not related, such as your pen-friend's mother, in which cases use **vous.**

Layout
1   You put only the name of your town and the date at the top of the letter, on the right.
2   You put your complete address on the back of the envelope, at the top, preceded by **Exp.,** which is short for **expéditeur** (sender).

Beginnings
1   To someone older than you: **Cher Monsieur** or **Chère Madame.**
2   To someone your own age: **Cher Pierre** or **Chère Marie, Mon cher Pierre** or **Ma chère Marie, Cher ami** or **Chère amie.**
3   To relations: **Mon cher oncle** or **Ma chère tante, Bien chers parents.**

Endings
1   To someone older than you: **Sincères salutations, Salutations distinguées.**
2   To someone your own age: **Amitiés, Amicalement, Cordialement, Bien à toi, A bientôt.**
3   To someone of whom you are very fond: **Bons baisers, Je t'embrasse, Affectueusement.**

Formal letters are those written to an office, an important person, to someone whom you know in a business capacity or to someone whom you do not know very well. In these letters the person you are writing to is always addressed as **vous.**

Layout
1   You put your full address and the date at the top of the letter, on the right.
2   You put the name and address of the person to whom you are writing at the top of the letter, on the left.

Beginnings
1   For a very formal letter (such as a business letter): **Monsieur** or **Madame.**
2   For a semi-formal letter (to someone older than you, whom you do not know well): **Cher Monsieur** or **Chère Madame.**

Endings
1   For a very formal letter: **Veuillez agréer, Madame (Monsieur), l'expression de mes sentiments distingués.**
2   For a semi-formal letter: **Veuillez croire, cher Monsieur (chère Madame), à mes sentiments les meilleurs,** or **Je vous prie d'accepter l'expression de mes sentiments les meilleurs.**

Informal letters

1. Accepting an invitation

Je $\begin{array}{l}te\\vous\end{array}$ remercie de Thank you for Je ne sais comment $\begin{array}{l}te\\vous\end{array}$ remercier de I don't know how to thank you for	$\begin{array}{l}ta\\votre\end{array}$ lettre your letter $\begin{array}{l}ta\\votre\end{array}$ carte postale your postcard	qui m'a fait grand plaisir which I was very pleased to get que je viens de recevoir which I have just received

J'aimerais beaucoup venir passer I'd like to come very much to spend	le mois d'août the month of August quelques jours a few days	chez $\begin{array}{l}toi\\vous\end{array}$ with you

Nous sommes en vacances We are on holiday	à partir du from	30 juin 30th June 20 juillet 20th July 1er août 1st August

Je peux I can Je pourrai I shall be able to Je pourrais I could	venir come	en bateau by boat par le train by train en avion by air

le 2 juillet on the 2nd July le 22 juillet on the 22nd July le 3 août on the 3rd August	et retourner chez moi and return home	une semaine a week quinze jours a fortnight un mois a month	plus tard later

Veux-tu Voulez-vous	revenir en Angleterre avec moi? Do you want to return to England with me?

Bordeaux, le 7 février

Chère Sarah, Je te remercie beaucoup de ta lettre, qui m'a fait grand plaisir. J'aimerais beaucoup aller en Angleterre l'année prochaine. Tu es très gentille de m'inviter. Je peux venir à partir du seize juillet. Est-ce que tu voudrais revenir en France avec moi? Nous pouvons passer une quinzaine en Angleterre, et une quinzaine en France, si ça te plaît.
Écris-moi pour me dire ce que tu en penses.

Amitiés,
Marie-France

Exercise 1

Your French pen-friend has just invited you to spend a month at his/her home in the summer. Write, accepting the invitation.

Exercise 2

Your French pen-friend has invited you to the seaside for a week at Easter. Write accepting, and saying why you will be especially pleased to go.

2. Inviting a friend to stay

J'écris pour *vous* / *te* demander si *vous pouvez* / *tu peux* I am writing to ask if you can **Est-ce que** *vous pouvez* / *tu peux* Can you	**venir passer** come and spend	**une semaine** a week **une quinzaine** a fortnight **un mois** a month

chez moi at my home	**l'année prochaine** next year **en été** in summer **au mois de juillet** in July **à Pâques** at Easter **à Noël** at Christmas

Je peux I can **Je pourrais** I could	**venir** *vous* / *te* **chercher** come and meet you	**à la gare de . . .** at the station at . . . **à Londres** in London **à Douvres** in Dover

Nous pouvons We can **Nous pourrions** We could **Nous pourrons** We shall be able to **Nous allons** We are going to	**aller au bord de la mer** go to the seaside **aller au cinéma** go to the cinema **aller nager** go swimming **jouer au tennis** play tennis **faire des promenades** go for walks

J'aimerais beaucoup *vous* / *te* **revoir** I should very much like to see you again

Je pourrais I could	**retourner en France avec** *vous* / *toi* return to France with you

Voulez-vous / *Veux-tu* Will you	**m'écrire bientôt pour me dire** write soon to tell me	**si** *vous êtes* / *tu es* **d'accord** if you agree

Amicalement Best wishes **Amitiés** With love

Londres, le 6 décembre

Mon cher Jacques,

Merci beaucoup pour ta lettre, que je viens de recevoir. Je t'écris à la hâte pour te demander si tu veux venir passer un mois chez nous l'année prochaine? Maman a dit qu'elle veut bien te recevoir, et ça me ferait grand plaisir. Nous pourrions passer des vacances très agréables ici. Le trente juillet, nous allons passer une semaine au bord de la mer. Puis après, nous pourrions faire des promenades en voiture aux environs de Londres. Nous pourrions aller nager à la piscine et jouer au tennis.

Je pourrais te rencontrer à Londres à la gare ou bien à l'aéroport, et nous pourrions rentrer à la maison en auto.

Veux-tu m'écrire bientôt pour me dire ce que tu en penses?

Amicalement
Peter.

Exercise 1

Invite your French pen-friend to stay with you at Easter next year. Suggest what entertainment you could offer.

Exercise 2

Invite your French pen-friend to stay at Christmas, and describe what you would do at Christmas-time.

Exercise 3

Invite your French pen-friend to come and stay for a fortnight, for some special occasion, such as a party or visit.

3. Refusing an invitation

Je te / vous remercie beaucoup de Thank you very much for	ta / votre lettre your letter ton / votre invitation your invitation	et de m'avoir invité(e) à and for having invited me to

faire un séjour chez toi / vous   stay with you   **venir en France**   come to France
aller au bord de la mer   go to the seaside

Malheureusement, je ne peux pas accepter, car . . .
Unfortunately, I cannot accept because . . .
Je suis très ennuyé(e) d'être forcé(e) de refuser mais . . .
I am very embarrassed to have to refuse but . . .

Je n'ai pas assez d'argent   I haven't enough money

Mon père / Ma mère   **est malade**   My father/My mother is ill

---

J'ai déjà promis d'aller I have already promised to go	**en Ecosse avec mes amis** to Scotland with my friends **chez ma tante** to my aunt's **en Espagne avec mon ami(e) et ses parents** to Spain with my friend and his /her parents

---

Est-ce qu'il serait possible de Would it be possible to	**remettre à plus tard cette visite?** postpone this visit? **venir à Noël?** come at Christmas? **venir à Pâques?** come at Easter? **venir en été?** come in summer?

Pardonne(z)-moi   Forgive me   **Je suis désolé(e)**   I'm very sorry

Calais, le 4 mars

Cher David,

J'écris à la hâte pour t'annoncer une triste nouvelle - je ne peux pas venir te rendre visite à Pâques. Je sais que tout est arrangé - je suis désolé - et je suis très ennuyé d'être forcé de refuser ton invitation.

Ma mère s'est cassé la jambe, et elle doit se reposer pendant quelques semaines. J'ai deux frères et deux sœurs, comme tu sais, et grand-maman habite chez nous aussi. Il y a donc beaucoup à faire, et mon père ne peut pas se débrouiller tout seul.

Si tu voyais ce que j'apprends à faire! Je ne savais pas qu'il y avait tant à faire. Je fais la vaisselle, je fais la lessive, je fais les courses, je fais la cuisine même.

Est-ce qu'il serait possible de venir au mois de juillet? J'aimerais beaucoup te revoir.

Rappelle-moi au bon souvenir de tes parents, et dis-leur que je suis très déçu. J'espère les revoir en été.

Ton ami,   Marc

Exercise 1

Your French pen-friend has invited you to France. Write, refusing the invitation, and saying why you cannot go.

Exercise 2

You have to cancel a trip to the theatre or cinema at the last moment. Write, apologising, and saying why.

4. A thank-you letter

Merci beaucoup pour le (la) Thank you very **Je te remercie beaucoup du (de la)** much for the		**cadeau** present **disque** record **lettre** letter **photo** photo	
que je viens de recevoir that I have just received		**J'aime beaucoup . . .** I am very fond of . . .	
et celui-ci (celle-ci) est particulièrement and this one is particularly		**intéressant(e)** interesting **amusant(e)** amusing **beau (belle)** beautiful **utile** useful	

Tu es très gentil(le) de It is very nice of you to	**penser à moi** think of me **l'avoir envoyé(e)** have sent it

La semaine prochaine, je vais t'envoyer Next week, I'll send you

une photo a photo **un disque** a record **un livre** a book **une revue** a magazine	**Quelles sortes de** What sort of	**photos** photos **disques** records **livres** books **revues** magazines

aimes-tu? do you like?	**Je te remercie encore** Thank you again.

Exercise 1

Write a thank-you letter to your French pen-friend, who has sent you something you particularly wanted for Christmas.

Exercise 2

Write a thank-you letter to your French pen-friend, who has sent you something (e.g. cheese, wine, brochures) which particularly represent his/her region of France. Ask some questions about what he/she has sent, and send him/her something suitable in return.

> Paris, le 5 janvier
>
> Chère Agnès,
>
> Je te remercie beaucoup de la charmante photo de ta famille que je viens de recevoir. Tu es très gentille de l'avoir envoyée. Maintenant je pourrai t'imaginer 'en famille'. Le bébé est absolument mignon. Quel âge a-t-il? Est-ce que vous étiez en vacances? Où avez-vous passé les vacances?
>
> Je veux t'envoyer un disque anglais, mais je ne sais pas quels chanteurs tu préfères. Écris-moi pour me le dire.
>
> Ton amie,
>
> Deborah.

Formal letters

5. Requesting information

Je vous prie de Je vous serais obligé(e) de	Would you please	m'envoyer des informations sur	send me some information about	la ville de (Boulogne) the town of (Boulogne)
Voulez-vous m'envoyer Veuillez m'envoyer	Will you send me	un tarif a price list des brochures some brochures une liste d'hôtels a list of hotels une liste de restaurants a list of restaurants un plan de la ville a map of the town		s'il vous plaît? please?
Je voudrais également savoir . . . I should also like to know . . .		à quelle heure les magasins ouvrent et ferment what time the shops open and close quels sont les jours de marché which are the market days quels sont les spécialités du pays what are the regional specialities		
Vous trouverez ci-inclus Please find enclosed			une enveloppe pour la réponse an envelope for reply un coupon-réponse international an international reply coupon	

Avec mes remerciements anticipés Thanking you in advance	je vous prie d'agréer Monsieur (Madame) I beg you to accept, Sir (Madam)

l'expression de mes sentiments distingués   my best wishes

Exercise 1

Write to a French seaside resort, requesting brochures, etc., and asking if there are any cinemas or discothèques.

Exercise 2

Write to a French scenic beauty spot, asking for brochures and maps, and asking if there is a youth hostel in the town.

Exercise 3

Write to the **Syndicat d'Initiative** in Calais requesting a map of the town. Ask also for information on restaurants, market days, opening and closing times of the shops, and availability of regional specialities, e.g. fish.

```
                                    14, Linden Rd,
                                    London, E.11
                                    le 10 mars

Syndicat d'Initiative,
BOULOGNE,
France;


Monsieur,

     Je vous serais très obligée de m'envoyer des
informations sur la ville de Boulogne;  Veuillez
m'envoyer des brochures, un plan de la ville, et
une liste d'hôtels, s'il vous plaît;  Je voudrais
également savoir s'il y a des monuments
historiques aux environs.

     Vous trouverez ci-inclus une enveloppe pour
la réponse.

     Avec mes remerciements anticipés, je vous
prie d'agréer, Monsieur, l'expression de mes
sentiments distingués;

                    Mary Brown

              Mary Brown (Miss)
```

6. A Complaint

| J'ai le regret de vous informer que   I regret to inform you that |

| je ne suis pas tout à fait satisfait(e) de
I am not entirely satisfied with
je ne suis pas du tout satisfait(e) de
I am not at all satisfied with
j'ai à me plaindre de
I have to complain about
je suis très fâché(e) contre vous de
I am very angry with you about | mon séjour
my stay | à votre hôtel
at your hotel
à votre camping
at your camp site
à votre villa
at your villa |

| Cela ne répondait aucunement à mon attente   I was very disappointed with it |

| Le service   The service | n'était pas très bon   was not very good
était affreux   was awful | |

| Les garçons
The waiters
Les femmes de chambre
The chambermaids | n'étaient pas très
were not very | capables   efficient
honnêtes   honest
poli(e)s   polite |

| Le terrain était   The ground was
La cuisine était   The kitchen was
Les cabinets étaient   The toilets were
La salle de bain était   The bathroom was
Les pièces étaient   The rooms were
Les chambres étaient   The bedrooms were | inondé(e)(s)   flooded
sale(s)   dirty
en désordre   untidy |

| Nous étions à court de   We were short of | couvertures   blankets   serviettes   towels
assiettes   plates   couteaux   knives
fourchettes   forks |

| Nous avons trouvé des
We found some | trous   holes
pistes d'escargot   snail tracks
perce-oreilles   earwigs
punaises   bugs
cafards   cockroaches | dans la tente   in the tent
dans la cuisine   in the kitchen
sur le tapis   on the carpet
dans le placard   in the cupboard
dans les lits   in the beds |

| La cuisinière   The oven
Le robinet   The tap
Le poste de télévision   The TV
L'électricité   The electricity
Le gaz   The gas | ne marchait pas   wasn't working |

| J'espère que vous ne tarderez pas à   I hope that you will not delay in |

| me donner satisfaction   sending a satisfactory reply
me rembourser le prix du séjour   repaying the cost of the stay
me rembourser une partie du prix   repaying part of the cost |

| Si non, je me verrai obligé(e) de   If not, I am afraid I shall have to |

| m'adresser   get in touch | aux agents   with the agents
au médecin de la santé   with the medical officer of health
au bureau de tourisme   with the tourist office
à mon notaire   with my solicitor |

| Ending: Veuillez agréer, Monsieur, mes salutations distinguées. |

Monsieur A. Villemar,
Directeur,
Hôtel Miramar,
Monte Carlo.

24, rue Robespierre,
75 – PARIS

le 5 septembre

Monsieur,

J'ai le regret de vous informer que je ne suis pas du tout satisfait de mon séjour à votre hôtel. L'eau n'était jamais chaude, on n'a jamais servi les repas à l'heure, et les garçons n'étaient pas du tout polis. En plus, j'ai le regret de vous dire qu'on m'a volé ma montre. C'est un "Oméga", en or, no. 3764. Je l'ai laissée sur la table de toilette la veille de mon départ, à huit heures du soir. A minuit, elle n'était plus là. Je croyais que ma femme l'avait mise dans son sac, mais non.

Je vous serais obligé de faire les recherches nécessaires. Si vous ne me donnez pas satisfaction, je me verrai obligé de m'adresser à la police.

Veuillez agréer, Monsieur, mes salutations distinguées.

Henri Juste

Henri Juste

Exercise 1

Write to a hotel complaining about your stay there. You may wish to complain about the service/ the rooms/ the amenities/ the meals. You may threaten to complain to your solicitors/ the Tourist Board.

Exercise 2

Write to the manager of a camp site, complaining about the difficulties you experienced there. Were you short of accommodation/ water/ calor gas? Were the toilets/ paths/ leisure facilities satisfactory? Would you complain to the Tourist Board/ the Health Officer?

Exercise 3

Write to the owner of a villa you rented, complaining about your uncomfortable stay there. Consider the cleanliness/ comfort and warmth/ provision of blankets, linen and kitchen equipment/ space and amenities. Would you complain to the agents/ your solicitors/ the Tourist Board?

7. Applying for a job

J'ai lu dans les petites annonces I read in the advertisements	**du journal . . .** of the newspaper . . .

que vous demandez that you require	**une secrétaire** a secretary **un(e) baby-sitter** a baby-sitter **un(e) au pair** an **au pair** **un vendeur/une vendeuse** a shop assistant **un moniteur/une monitrice** a helper/play-group leader

Je suis très intéressé(e) par ce poste, car This post appeals to me very much, because	**J'aime beaucoup les enfants** I like children very much	
	j'aimerais beaucoup travailler I would very much like to work	**dans un bureau** in an office **dans un magasin** in a shop **dans une épicerie** in a grocer's

Donc, je me permets de vous offrir mes services   Therefore, I should like to apply for this post
C'est pour cette raison que je postule la place que vous offrez
This is why I should like to apply for the post you offer

Pour connaître mes aptitudes comme employé(e) je vous prie de vous adresser à . . .
For a reference, please apply to . . .

Je vous prie de bien vouloir trouver ci-joint Please find enclosed	**une copie de mon diplôme** a copy of my diploma **une lettre du directeur (de la directrice)** **de mon collège** a letter from my headmaster/ headmistress

Ending: **Espérant que vous prendrez ma demande en considération, je vous prie,**
        Monsieur/Madame, d'accepter mes sentiments les meilleurs.

68, rue Voltaire,
71-MACON,
France.

le 8 novembre

Madame E. Delille,
44, rue Flaubert,
71-MACON.

Madame,

Me référant à votre annonce parue ce matin dans le Figaro, j'ai l'honneur de solliciter l'emploi d'assistante dans votre magasin. Je suis très intéressée par ce poste, car l'année dernière, je travaillais dans une boulangerie tous les samedis, et c'est un travail que j'ai trouvé très intéressant.

J'ai seize ans, et j'ai passé huit matières pour mon Baccalauréat dont j'ai réussi sept. Pour connaître mes aptitudes comme employée, je vous prie de vous adresser à la boulangère, Madame Christine Verlaine, dont l'adresse est 22, rue du Marché, Macon.

Je vous prie de bien vouloir trouver ci-joint une lettre du directeur de mon collège.

Veuillez agréer, Madame, l'expression de mes sentiments respectueux.

Anne-Marie Guerlain

Exercise 1

Apply for a job as au pair, asking what your duties would be.

Exercise 2

Imagine you are a French boy or girl applying to be a **moniteur** or **monitrice** in a French **colonie de vacances.** Say why you would like the post, and why you think you would be suitable.

8. Writing about lost property

Le 2 septembre 1980, j'ai remis au bureau de poste à Reims
On 2nd September 1980 I posted . . . at Rheims

une lettre a letter **un paquet recommandé** a registered parcel	**dont le destinataire était** addressed to	**M. Jean Loup,** **10, rue Victor Hugo,** **Marseilles**

Cette lettre/Ce paquet n'est pas arrivé(e) à destination   This letter/This parcel did not arrive

J'espère que vous ne tarderez pas à faire les recherches **nécessaires** I hope you will not delay in making the necessary enquiries	**Veuillez agréer, Monsieur,** **l'expression de mes sentiments** **les meilleurs** Yours faithfully,

	j'ai passé la nuit dans votre hôtel I spent the night at your hotel		
Le 2 septembre **1980** On 2nd September 1980	**je suis allé(e) à** **votre cinéma/théâtre** I went to you cinema/theatre	**J'avais** I had	**une place au balcon** a seat in the circle **un fauteuil d'orchestre** a seat in the stalls

Là, There,	**j'ai perdu** I lost **on m'a volé** somebody stole **j'ai laissé** I left	**ma valise** my case **mon parapluie** my umbrella **ma montre** my watch **une bague** a ring **un manteau** a coat

C'est	**une montre** **une bague**	**de grande valeur**	It is a valuable watch/ring	**marqué(e) à mon nom** with my name on it

Je vous serais reconnaissant(e)   I should be grateful if you
de bien vouloir faire les   would kindly make
recherches nécessaires   the necessary enquiries

Monsieur le Directeur,
Bureau des Objets Trouvés,
Calais

112, rue Baudelaire,
75 - PARIS, 14e

le 30 août

Monsieur,

Le 23 août, j'ai pris le train de 8.00 heures de Calais à Paris, et, malheureusement, j'ai laissé ma serviette dans le train. C'est une serviette en cuir brun, qui contient des lettres et des papiers divers signée de mon nom.

Je vous serais reconnaissant de bien vouloir faire les recherches nécessaires, et de m'écrire dès que vous aurez des nouvelles. J'ai déjà fait des recherches à Paris, mais sans succès.

Je crois que j'étais dans le troisième wagon, mais je n'en suis pas sûr. C'était un compartiment de deuxième classe.

Je vous remercie d'avance et vous prie de croire à l'expression de mes sentiments distingués.

Marc Lasourde

Exercise 1

Write to a Post Office at Nice about a registered parcel which has not arrived at its destination.

Exercise 2

Write to a hotel about a ring which you think you left on the dressing table.

Exercise 3

Write to a hotel complaining that someone stole a coat out of your car during the night.

9. Booking at a hotel or a camp site

J'ai l'intention de I intend **Je désire** I wish **Je voudrais** I should like	**passer une semaine** to spend a week **passer deux jours** to spend two days

à votre hôtel at your hotel **au camping à** at the camp site at . . . **à l'auberge de jeunesse à** . . . at the Youth Hostel at . . .	**à partir du** . . . starting from . . .

Je voudrais retenir une chambre I'd like to book a room	**à un lit** with one bed **pour deux personnes** for two **à deux lits** with twin beds **avec douche** with a shower **avec salle de bains** with a bathroom

Avez-vous un emplacement de libre pour Have you room for	**une tente?** a tent? **une caravane?** a caravan?

Nous prendrons We shall have	**la pension complète** full board **la demi-pension** half board
à 30 francs 40 francs (at a particular price) 50 francs	**par jour par personne** each daily

Nous arriverons We shall arrive **Nous repartirons** We shall leave	**le deux août à midi** 2nd August at noon **à 14h.** at 2 p.m. **à 16h.** at 4 p.m.

J'aimerais savoir I would like to know **Quels sont** What are	**vos prix tout compris** your "all-in" prices **vos tarifs** your prices
J'attends confirmation de votre part I await your confirmation	

Exercise 1

Write to a youth hostel, booking for three days, for three people (state the sex), from 10th September.

Exercise 2

Write to a hotel, booking, for a month, one double and one single room, with bathrooms, from 1st August. Ask if they can accommodate your dog.

Exercise 3

Write to a camp site, booking for a week, for two tents, from 5th June.

23, rue Rivoli,
Paris, 6e,
le 3 mai

Monsieur P. Dupont,
Directeur,
Hôtel Beaux-Arts,
67 STRASBOURG.

Monsieur,

J'ai l'intention de passer une semaine à Strasbourg à partir du quatre juin. Je voudrais retenir une chambre à votre hôtel; Avez-vous une chambre à un lit, avec salle de bain? Je prendrai la pension complète.

J'arriverai à 11.00 heures le 4 juin, et je repartirai à 14.00 heures le 11 juin.

J'attends confirmation de votre part, et j'aimerais savoir vos tarifs.

Veuillez agréer, Monsieur, l'expression de mes sentiments distingués.

Ali Mohammed.

Section 4
Letters to answer

Replying to letters is sometimes more difficult than it appears. One problem can be identifying all the points which need an answer. Often, of course, the questions are obvious, beginning with a recognizable question word such as **quand** or **où**, and ending with a question mark. Sometimes though, the query is put differently – in the form of a statement, a command or a gentle hint – and as a result may well be overlooked. Note for example the following phrases which will require an answer:

Vous seriez bien gentil de . . .	It would be very kind of you to . . .
Veuillez me faire savoir . . .	Kindly let me know . . .
Veux-tu bien . .?	Will you please . .?
Je veux savoir . . .	I want to know . . .
J'écris pour vous demander . .	I am writing to ask you . . .
Dis-moi . . .	Tell me . . .
Parle-moi de . . .	Tell me about . . .
Raconte-moi . . .	Tell me . . .
Je peux vous offrir un prix très intéressant . . .	I can offer you a very competitive price . . .

However, answering all the relevant points is not normally all you do when replying to a letter. In a reply to a pen-friend, for example, you would probably want to include some questions of your own. This aspect of your letter is, in fact, one of the main ingredients which help the correspondence continue. Below is a list of question words for you to refer to when composing your own questions.

Est-ce que . .?	(This turns any statement into a question)
Qu'est-ce que . . ?	What . . ?
Quel (les) . . ?	Which . . ?
Quand est-ce que . . ?	When . . ?
Où est-ce-que . . ?	Where . . ?
Pourquoi . . ?	Why . . ?
Comment . . ?	How . . ?
A quelle heure . . ?	At what time . . ?

1. Details about yourself

Menton, le 2 septembre

Cher John,

Je suis très heureux d'avoir reçu ton adresse de mon professeur de français. Je veux bien correspondre avec toi. Quel âge as-tu? Moi, J'ai quinze ans. Quelle est la date de ton anniversaire? As-tu des frères ou des sœurs? Comment s'appellent-ils? Quel âge ont-ils? Moi, J'ai une sœur, âgée de dix-sept ans, qui s'appelle Anne-Marie.

Depuis combien de temps apprends-tu le français? Aimes-tu les cours de français? Moi, J'apprends l'anglais depuis trois ans, et ça me plaît beaucoup. Mon prof est assez sympa. Qu'est-ce que tu aimes comme sport? Moi J'aime bien la natation et le football. Aimes-tu la musique moderne, et les discos? Dis-moi tes goûts. Moi, J'apprends à jouer de la guitare et ça me plaît beaucoup. Le weekend je vais chez des copains écouter des disques ou jouer aux cartes.

Comment est la ville où tu habites? Menton se trouve au bord de la mer

J'attends la réponse.
Ton nouvel ami,
Paul.

Exercise 1

Paul wants to know quite a lot about his new friend. Make a list, in English, of all the things he wants John to tell him.

Exercise 2

Now answer Paul's questions in French, as if you were John.
1. Quel âge as-tu? (J'ai......... ans)
2. Quelle est la date de ton anniversaire? (La date de mon anniversaire est.........)
3. As-tu des frères ou des sœurs? (J'ai...... frère(s) et...... sœur(s)/ Je n'ai pas de....../ Je suis fils/ fille unique)
4. Comment s'appellent-ils? (Mon frère s'appelle........., et ma sœur s'appelle.........)
5. Quel âge ont-ils? (Mon frère a......... ans et ma sœur a...... ans)
6. Depuis combien de temps apprends-tu le français? (J'apprends le français depuis.........ans)
7. Aimes-tu les cours de français? (J'aime....../ Je n'aime pas......)
8. Qu'est-ce que tu aimes comme sport? (J'aime......)
9. Aimes-tu la musique moderne, et les discos? (J'aime beaucoup....../ Je n'aime pas....../ Je n'aime ni......... ni.........)
10. Dis-moi tes goûts. (J'aime bien........./ Je préfère......)
11. Comment est la ville où tu habites? (La ville où j'habite est......)

Exercise 3

What do we find out about Paul from his letter?

2. Applying for an **au pair** post

Paris, le 24 avril

Chère Mademoiselle,

Je vous remercie de votre lettre. Vous êtes désireuse de travailler au pair pendant les grandes vacances, n'est-ce pas? Veuillez me faire connaître les détails suivants. Quel âge avez-vous? Avez-vous des frères ou des sœurs? Pourquoi avez-vous choisi cet emploi en particulier? Quels sont vos passe-temps préférés? Aimez-vous faire des promenades? Savez-vous nager? Savez-vous conduire une auto? Savez-vous faire la cuisine? Quelles sortes de repas savez-vous préparer pour les enfants? Finalement, veuillez me faire savoir la date où vous pourriez venir en France.
Veuillez agréer, Mademoiselle, l'expression de mes sentiments distingués.

Henriette Labiche

Exercise 1

Make a list, in English, of all the questions that Madame Labiche asks the prospective **au pair** girl.

Exercise 2

Now answer the following questions, in French, pretending that you are the applicant for the post.
1. Vous êtes désireuse de trouver une place **au pair** pendant les grandes vacances, n'est-ce pas? (Oui, je suis désireuse.........)
2. Quel âge avez-vous? (J'ai......... ans)
3. Avez-vous des frères ou des sœurs? (J'ai.........)
4. Pourquoi avez-vous choisi cet emploi en particulier? (J'ai choisi cet emploi car...... je voudrais améliorer mon français/ j'aime les enfants/ j'ai envie de visiter Paris/ j'ai besoin de gagner de l'argent)
5. Quels sont vos passe-temps préférés? (Mes passe-temps préférés sont...... la natation/ la couture/ la lecture)
6. Aimez-vous faire des promenades? (J'aime beaucoup....../ Je n'aime pas.........)
7. Savez-vous nager? (Je sais....../ Je ne sais pas....../ Je vais apprendre à......)
8. Savez-vous conduire une auto?
9. Savez-vous faire la cuisine?
10. Quelles sortes de plats savez-vous préparer? (Je sais préparer...... de la soupe/ des omelettes/ du ragoût/ de la compote de fruits)
11. Veuillez me faire savoir la date où vous pourriez venir en France. (Je pourrais venir.........)

3. At home after the holidays

Brest, le 3 Septembre

Chère Suzanne,

Je te prie de m'excuser de ne pas avoir écrit plus tôt. C'est que ma tante Sophie m'a invitée à l'imprévu à passer une semaine à Paris. Je suis rentrée chez moi samedi seulement.

Je me suis bien amusée à Paris. Samedi soir je suis sortie avec ma tante dîner à "L'escargot d'or", restaurant très chic près de la Seine; puis nous sommes allées au théâtre voir ce fameux groupe américain dont tout le monde parle - "Les Doulidous". C'était sensas!

Nous avons fait des promenades, en auto et à pied, et j'ai pris beaucoup de photos. Mardi nous avons fait une promenade en bateau-mouche sur la Seine, ce qui était très intéressant et après cela nous avons fait du lèche-vitrine,

Et toi, as-tu passé de bonnes vacances? Es-tu allée au bord de la mer ou à la campagne? Es-tu allée avec tes parents ou avec des copains? Est-ce qu'il faisait beau temps? Quand tu m'écriras, il faudra me dire tout ce que tu as fait.

Bons baisers
Marie

Exercise 1

Make a list, in English, of the questions asked by Marie.

Exercise 2

Write a reply to Marie's letter, making sure you answer all her questions.

Exercise 3

What do we find out about Marie's stay in Paris from her letter?

4. A letter from a new pen-friend

Bordeaux, le 2 décembre

Ma chère Suzanne,

Je te remercie bien de ta deuxième lettre, qui m'a fait grand plaisir. Tu as dit que ta mère a été malade. Qu'est-ce qu'elle avait? Comment va-t-elle maintenant? Quand elle était au lit, as-tu dû faire le ménage? Qu'est-ce que tu as dû faire? Moi je déteste faire le ménage - mon frère aussi - mais quelquefois nous faisons les commissions ensemble quand même.

Que fais-tu pendant tes loisirs? Aimes-tu le sport, ou préfères-tu aller aux discos? Moi, je m'intéresse à la natation.

Est-ce que tu passes des examens à présent à l'école? Quelles matières préfères-tu? Lesquelles est-ce que tu n'aimes pas? Moi j'aime bien la géographie, mais je préfère la biologie et les maths.

Tu serais bien gentille de m'envoyer une photo. Que vas-tu faire à Noël? Moi je pars en vacances de neige.

Je te quitte maintenant,

Bons baisers,

Anne-Marie

Exercise 1

Make a list, in English, of the information Anne-Marie would like.

Exercise 2

Write a reply to Anne-Marie's letter, answering all her questions. Add some questions of your own. Here are some examples to start you off:

Tout le monde va bien chez toi?
Tu ne m'as pas parlé de ton frère. Quel âge a-t-il?
Va-t-il au même collège que toi?
Est-ce que tu t'intéresses à la musique pop?
Aimes-tu . . . danser/ écouter des disques?
Avec qui est-ce que tu pars en vacances?
Sais-tu déjà faire du ski?

Exercise 3

What do we find out about Anne-Marie from her letter?

5. Describing the household duties of an **au pair**

> 11 Hands Road,
> Birmingham.
> le 3 mai.
>
> Chère Madame,
>
> Je vous remercie beaucoup de votre gentille lettre à laquelle je m'empresse de répondre. Je serai très contente de passer le mois août chez vous comme 'au pair.' Voulez-vous bien me renseigner sur cet emploi?
>
> Combien d'enfants avez-vous, et quel âge ont-ils? Est-ce qu'il faut faire le ménage, ou tout simplement garder les enfants? Est-ce que les enfants aiment faire des promenades? Aiment-ils les sports? A quelle heure se lèvent-ils? Va-t-on faire des excursions?
>
> Je vous prie d'agréer, Madame l'expression de mes sentiments respectueux.
>
> Margaret Brown

Exercise 1

Make a list, in English, of the questions asked by Margaret.

Exercise 2

Write a reply to Margaret's letter, as though you are the mother of the children. Be sure to answer all the questions, and add two or three of your own. Here are some examples to start you off:

C'est la première fois que vous travaillez comme **au pair**?
Est-ce que vous voudrez parler anglais ou français?
Savez-vous l'heure exacte de votre arrivée?
Est-ce que vous prendrez le bateau et le train ou l'avion?

5. Describing a holiday

Soissons, le 2 mai.

Mon cher Stephen, Merci bien pour ta lettre. J'ai été bien content de recevoir de tes nouvelles.

Tu me dis que tu es allé passer une semaine chez ta tante, mais tu ne me donnes pas de détails. Dis-moi, où habite-t-elle ? Au bord de la mer, ou en ville ? A-t-elle des enfants de ton âge ? Qu'est-ce que tu as fait pour t'amuser ? Es-tu sorti seul ? Est-ce que tu as pu pratiquer des sports ? Lesquels ?

Moi, je suis resté chez moi pendant les vacances de Pâques, mais je ne me suis pas du tout ennuyé. J'ai fait une excursion à Paris, et d'autres à la campagne avec mes amis. Nous avons fait des promenades à vélo: As-tu un vélo ? Fais-tu des promenades quelquefois ?

Écris-moi bientôt.

Ton copain,

Henri

Write a reply to Henri's letter, making sure you answer all his questions, and adding a few of your own. Here are some examples of the sort of questions you could ask:

Qu'est-ce que tu as vu à Paris?
As-tu visité le centre Pompidou?
Es-tu monté à la Tour Eiffel?
Est-ce que tu t'es promené dans le Quartier Latin?
Où es-tu allé à vélo?
Combien coûte un vélo en France?

7. Going to New York

Paris, le 2 juin

Cher David,

Je te remercie beaucoup de ta lettre. Tu as de la chance, n'est-ce pas, d'aller faire un séjour aux États-Unis? Tu ne m'as pas parlé de ton oncle qui habite à New York. Comment est-il?

Qu'est-ce que tu comptes faire aux États-Unis? Quels monuments historiques veux-tu voir? Ou préfères-tu visiter les cinémas et les discos? Vas-tu acheter beaucoup de disques? Vas-tu voir des matchs de basketball? Sais-tu jouer au basketball?

Combien de temps vas-tu passer aux États-Unis? Tu ne veux pas de compagnon, par hasard? Je serais très content de t'accompagner! — Non, c'est une blague. Cet été je vais passer les grandes vacances en colonie de vacances.

N'oublie pas de m'envoyer une carte postale de New York.

Ton copain Georges.

Write a reply to Georges' letter, making sure you answer all his questions, and adding a few of your own. You could ask, for example, what a **colonie de vacances** is, whom he is going with, how he will spend his time there, and so on.

8. Arranging a meeting

Write a reply to the following letter. It would be a good idea to find out from your correspondent the sort of thing he or she likes to do, before you meet.

Paris, le 8 mai.

chère Ann,

Je suis très heureuse car la date de mon départ pour l'Angleterre approche. Je vais prendre le train qui quitte Paris à 9 heures du matin et se compte arriver à Londres à 18 heures. Dis-moi, où est-ce que je dois t'attendre? Est-ce que c'est toi qui viendras me rencontrer, ou est-ce que tes parents viendront? Comment est-ce que je vais te reconnaître? — car j'ai perdu ta photo.

Tu seras gentille de m'envoyer ces détails et de me dire aussi ce que nous ferons pendant mon séjour chez toi.

Amitiés,
Paulette.

Gapped letters

For each letter, there are two tasks:

a   Write out the letter, replacing the signs by words. If there is no picture to guide you, you will have to read the rest of the sentence for clues. Sometimes you have some extra vocabulary at the end of the letter to give you more clues.
   When you find more than one dotted line in a gap, it is a hint that you probably need more than one word in the space. However, if you can find a sensible answer in one word, that is perfectly acceptable.
   When you have a picture clue, the answer may be one or more words.

b   Write a reply. Use your own name if you like. Try not to leave out any of the questions.

1.   A first letter: describing yourself and talking about your hobbies

Toulouse, le 9 novembre

Chere Tamsin,

Je suis vraiment très … de pouvoir correspondre avec une anglaise, … tout d'abord

je … améliorer mon anglais et puis j'espère … tu deviendras une tres bonne amie.

D'abord je … me décrire. , je … grande, j'ai les cheveux

 et bruns.

Maintenant je vais te décrire mes loisirs. J'aime … les sports. Je pratique le

 et la , mais j'aime bien aussi le , la

, le patin à glace. J'aime beaucoup aussi ,

 et je suis aussi assez gourmande!

Quels sont tes loisirs, tes goûts, ton aspect? Ecris-moi vite!

J'espère que l'on se rencontrera bientôt!

Au revoir

Antoinette

58

améliorer   to improve
l'aspect(m)   appearance
tu deviendras   you will become
gourmand(e)   fond of food

Quels sont tes goûts?(m)   What do you like doing?
les loisirs(m)   spare time activities
le patin à glace   ice skating

2.   **Talking about your family**

Montmorillon, le 4 octobre

Cher Dominic,

Je … Stéphane et je suis ton  français. Je suis de 3e au

Lycée-Collège Jean Moulin à Montmorillon. J'ai . La plus … s'appelle

Sandrine et elle **16** . La plus … s'appelle Emmanuelle, elle a 10 ans.

Mon , Gilbert, travaille à l'Equipment à Lussac-les-Châteaux. Ma mère est

. Elle … Marinette. Mon pere adore donc nous pourrons

faire un tournoi. Mes sont un peu ennuyeuses mais elles sont parfois

sympathiques. Nous avons , qui s'appelle Florence. Nous … de l'autre côté

de Montmorillon, mais nous sommes près des .

Où habites-tu? Combien de frères et sœurs as-tu? Qu'est-ce qu'ils aiment?

Au revoir

Stéphane

ennuyeux, ennuyeuse   annoying
parfois   sometimes
sympathique   njce, likeable
un tournoi   tournament

3. Home

Paris, le 12 juillet

Cher Howard,

Merci beaucoup … … …, qui m'a beaucoup . Tu m'as

– tu as ! Je ne savais pas que tu allais …

Est-ce que tu aimes Doncaster? Est-ce ou ? Est-ce que

tu habites ou un ? Est-ce que tu partages avec

… frère? Est-ce que tu as ou ?

Comment est l'école? Est-ce loin? Dis – … ce que tu penses de Doncaster.

Bien à toi,

Pierre

déménager   to move house   **déménagé**   moved house
étonner   to surprise   **étonné(e)**   surprised
plaire   to please   **ça m'a plu**   it pleased me

4. Describing a friend

Dijon, le 6 novembre

Bonjour,

Comment vas-tu? Connais-tu une jeune de ton entourage qui

aimerait une Française? Voilà le problème: j'ai une amie qui … Esmée et qui

voudrait avoir des contacts avec . Elle est brune, très mignonne. Les …

bleus, un fin, elle a tout pour plaire. Elle mesure environ 1 mètre 68 et est

élancée. Elle est âgée de 14 …, née le 19/06/ … Elle pratique le avec

passion, aime  voire pop, aime et surtout est très amusante.

Elle passe son temps à .

Je pense que tu trouveras une copine pour correspondre avec Esmée.

Ton amie,

Stéphanie

élancé(e) slender
de ton entourage from your circle of friends
mignon(ne) sweet, pretty
voire even

5. Part-time jobs and pocket money

Bordeaux, le 2 décembre

Cher ami,

Bonjour! Comment vas-tu? Merci pour ta gentille lettre, dans laquelle tu décris ton 'job'.

Chaque samedi en France pour gagner un peu j'ai un petit travail. Je fais du babysitting et distribue les .

Le matin je distribue les  de à . Cet emploi est très bien car il me permet d'avoir de l'argent de poche mais l'inconvénient c'est l'horaire.

Ensuite, le soir je fais du  à partir de jusqu'à environ , une heure. Quelquefois je reste toute 🌙☆ – cela dépend des personnes. Ce petit 'job' est très intéressant si les … sont sympa, autrement c'est assez embêtant.

Avec cet argent je m'achète [image essence] pour ma motocyclette et je mets le reste de l'argent à la [image CREDIT LYONNAIS].

Amitiés,

Gustave

In reply, you could describe your own job, and say how you spend your pocket money

autrement otherwise
embêtant unpleasant, annoying
un emploi job

environ about
l'horaire hours of work
sympa nice, likeable

6. School

Nancy, le 22 septembre

Cher ami,

Merci beaucoup pour ta lettre, dans laquelle tu décris la rentrée des classes. C'est

la rentrée pour nous aussi, hélas!

En , le jeudi est très chargé, nous … … cours … la journée:

  . Mais le

vendredi est super, on a trois heures d'études et des fois on finit ou

. Parfois il y a qui sont absents, alors … va en étude.

Le lundi c'est très dur car il faut à 7h et à

l'école à 8h pour commencer avec . On débouche à 5h ou 4h. On a plus de

devoirs que l'Angleterre. Quand sont les grandes vacances?

Bien à toi,

Simon

In reply you could describe your own week at school.

chargé   full
déboucher   to come out (of school)
parfois   sometimes
la rentrée des classes   beginning of term

7. Sport

Tours, le 8 avril

Cher ami,

Merci beaucoup pour ta lettre, dans laquelle tu décris tes passe-temps. Elle était

très ….

…, je suis très sportif, je passe presque tout mon temps … à … du sport.

En hiver, le lundi, le mardi, et … …, après les cours, je … 1 heure de

environ. Les autres …, c'est à dire le mercredi et le vendredi, je pratique

dans l'équipe de Tours. Le weekend est … chargé: championnat de et

tournois de .

En été j'aime bien et . Mais mon sport préféré, c'est

 , que je pratique pendant les … vacances.

Bien sûr, tout le … en France ne fait … autant de sports, il y en a qui préfère

Amitiés,

Paul

autant de as much, as many
le championnat championship
chargé busy, full
la planche à voile windsurfing
le tournoi tournament

A visit to the zoo

Paris, le 5 mai

Mon cher Howard,

Je te remercie de ta lettre, qui était très … . Tu dis que tu es allé au zoo la semaine

… . Moi, j'aime beaucoup … … . Dis-moi ce que tu as … . Où … … le zoo? **?**

y es-tu arrivé? Qu'est-ce que tu as … d'abord? Où as-tu ? En plein air ou

 ? Quels préfères-tu? Moi, je préfère . Tu dis

que tu as eu un petit accident près de la des . Qu'est-ce qui

s'est passé?

Comment vont tes ? Et ta ? Rappelle-moi à leurs bons

souvenirs.

Pierre

se passer   to happen

9. A trip to Paris

Lyon, le 20 avril

Ma chère amie,

Merci beaucoup pour ta lettre. Tu dis que tu es allée à Paris récemment. Quelle

chance! Est-ce que tu y es allée  ou ? Le trajet

a pris combien de temps? Tu as passé combien de ... à Paris? Qu'est-ce que tu as

? Es-tu allé ? Qu'est-ce que tu as ? Est-ce que

tu ... retourner a Paris l'année prochaine?

Affectueusement,

Susan

quelle chance! what good luck!
récemment recently
le trajet journey

10. At the seaside

Paris, le 12 juillet

Mon cher Howard,

Merci beaucoup pour ta lettre, qui m'a beaucoup plu. Tu as dit que tu as … une

journée 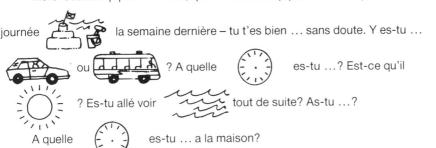 la semaine dernière – tu t'es bien … sans doute. Y es-tu …

ou ? A quelle es-tu …? Est-ce qu'il

? Es-tu allé voir tout de suite? As-tu …?

A quelle es-tu … a la maison?

Vas-tu faire d'autres excursions? Où veux-tu aller ensuite? Moi, je … faire une

excursion à Londres un de ces jours.

J'ai essayé de hier, mais je n'ai pas pu obtenir de réponse. Est-ce que

tu n'étais pas ? Qu'est-ce que tu faisais?

Ecris-moi bientôt.

Ton copain,

Pierre

Je suis I Tu es you	allé(e) went arrivé(e) arrived rentré(e) returned home
Je me suis I	amusé(e) had fun
J'ai I Tu as you	déjeuné had lunch nagé swam passé spent (time)

11. Arranging for a friend to come and stay

Lyon, le 20 juin

Chere Sarah,

Je suis très d' que tu … venir passer deux semaines

chez … au … de juillet. Je sais que tu n'as … encore pu obtenir une réservation, mais

quand tu l'auras, veux-tu bien m'  en me précisant le jour et de

ton arrivée? C'est mon oncle qui ira te … à la gare. Je vais lui donner de toi,

mais est-ce que tu … te distinguer de la foule en portant , par exemple,

ou , ou , ou quelquechose comme ça?

Je t'envoie une photo de mon … . Ses sont un peu … gris que dans

que dans le photo, et il est plus , mais je crois que tu le reconnaîtras quand

même.

Est-ce que tu as des **??? ** à me poser sur le séjour? N'oublie …

d'apporter – il va faire très au mois de … !

A bientôt,

Yvette

la foule crowd
par exemple for example
préciser to inform
quand même all the same
reconnaître to recognise

12. Thanking someone for a present

Paris, le 3 janvier

Cher Howard,

J'espère que tu as passé un joyeux . Je t'écris pour te … beaucoup

du très joli que tu m'as envoyé, qui m'a beaucoup plu.

Nous nous sommes bien amuśes à , car nous sommes allés

 dans les Pyrénées. C'était …! Est-ce que tu sais ? Quels

sont tes sports préférés?

Ensuite, nous avons passé par la ville d'Auch, où … ma tante. Nous y sommes

restés quelques jours. Est-ce que tu rends visite à tous les parents à Noël, comme nous?

Ecris-moi pour … … ce que tu as … pour t'amuser à Noël.

Bien à toi,

Pierre

ensuite   afterwards
rendre visite à   to visit

13. What are we going to do?

Guillon, le 6 février

Mon cher Paul,

… … pour ta lettre, dans laquelle tu confirmes que tes parents et …, vous voulez faire un échange de domicile avec nous au … d'août.

Je … que vous … amuserez bien à Guillon. On peut dans la piscine, (heureusement qu'il n'y a … beaucoup de), se promener dans et visiter les … … villages aux environs. Il y a une fête folklorique à Guillon à partir du 10 … et un concours de à Bratz le 14-15 qui va sûrement t'intéresser – je ne sais pas pour !

Tu serais gentil de nous … pour nous … ce qu'il y a comme activités régionales chez … au mois d'août. Est-ce qu' … … … des ou des villes … à visiter?

Amitiés,

Jacques

dans laquelle   in which
un échange de domicile   home exchange
une fête folklorique   country fair
activités régionales   local activities

14. Making a reservation at a hotel

3 rue de France
14450 Calvados
Normandie

le 19 avril

Monsieur,

Je … passer à Nice au mois de juillet. Un de mes amis m'a …

l'adresse de … hôtel. Je tiens à savoir inclusifs. Veuillez me faire savoir si

vous aurez vacante à partir du 4 juillet.

Veuillez agréer, monsieur, l'expression de mes sentiments distingués.

Jean Larue

Instead of replying, write a similar letter saying you wish to spend a week in a hotel at Marseille. You wish to know the prices, and you would like one room with one bed, and one room with two beds.

15. Making a reservation at a youth hostel

14 chemin des tignes
06100 Nice

le 3 mai

Monsieur,

Nous ... passer à Perpignan au mois d'août dans votre ...... de ......

Je tiens à savoir 〔sc〕 ? inclusifs. Veuillez me faire savoir si vous aurez de la

place pour 👥👥👥 à partir du 6 août.

Est-ce qu'on peut louer des ⬭⬭ ?

Veuillez agréer, monsieur, l'expression de mes sentiments distingués.

Elisabeth Sarrazin

Instead of replying, write a similar letter saying you wish to spend a week in a youth hostel at Biarritz. You wish to know the prices, and you would like to know if there are vacancies for three boys (or three girls).

16. Making a reservation at a camp site

142 blvd de Cessole
22000 St. Brieut
Bretagne

le 21 février

Monsieur,

Je vous … afin de vous demander de réserver des emplacements dans votre de Pinède pour les prochaines vacances d'été.

Pourriez-vous nous confirmer que la semaine du 18 au 24 juillet serait possible? Nous

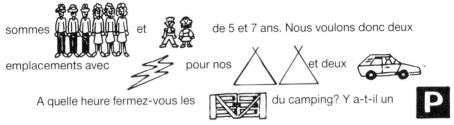

sommes [image] et [image] de 5 et 7 ans. Nous voulons donc deux

emplacements avec [image] pour nos [image] et deux [image].

A quelle heure fermez-vous les [image] du camping? Y a-t-il un

à l'extérieur?

Pouvez-vous, s'il vous plaît, nous envoyer des prospectus sur la [image] de

Biarritz en même temps que votre  ? Merci d'avance.

Veuillez agréer, monsieur, l'expression de mes sentiments distingués.

Claudine Pouilly

Instead of replying, write a similar letter booking a site at Dinard for a fortnight in August for a caravan. Ask if there is a self-service restaurant at the camp site.

Test Section

1 Read the following letter and then write to Dominique's friend Claude. Try to answer all the questions. Your letter should contain 50-60 words.

Quimper, le 30 avril

Salut,

Merci pour ta lettre. Mon ami Claude Evain et sa famille vont passer un an en Irlande du Nord parce que Monsieur Evain va travailler dans un hôpital près de chez toi. Claude va être élève à ton école et donc il cherche des renseignements. Quelle est la date de la rentrée? A quelle heure est-ce que les cours commencent et finissent? Comment est ton prof d'anglais? Comment est-ce qu'on s'amuse le weekend? Claude est assez gros et aime beaucoup les repas. Naturellement il veut savoir ce qu'on mange au petit déjeuner en Irlande du Nord.

Voici l'adresse de Claude. Ecris-lui en français s'il te plaît. Il est très faible en anglais.

CLAUDE EVAIN, 24 Rue du GENERAL PATTON, 38600 QUIMPER.

Amicalement,

DOMINIQUE

(Northern Ireland Schools Examinations Council, Basic Level, June 1988)

2 You have received a letter from your French pen-friend, asking about your home. Write a letter in French, in reply, and make sure you say:

– if you live in a house or a flat;
– what rooms there are;
– what your room is like;
– if you have a garden or not.

You will probably need to write about 60 words. There is no need to count the number of words.

(NEA, Basic Level, June 1988)

After your pen-friend Luc has gone back to France, you discover that you've lost a T-shirt. Write and ask him if he's got it, and if he could send it back to you. Tell him what it's like.

(Scottish Examination Board, Standard Grade, General Level)

A few weeks later, you go away for the day. You send Luc a postcard. Say where you are, what the weather's like, and that you hope to see him next year.

M LUC DUVAL
18 ROUTE DU LAC
ROUEN
FRANCE

(Scottish Examination Board, Standard Grade, General Level)

5   When you went to visit an elderly neighbour in France, Madame Vierzon, you received no reply. Looking through the window, you discovered that she was lying on the floor, having fallen and hurt her leg. Write a letter to Madame Ramel, Madame Vierzon's sister, explaining what has happened, how you obtained help for her and where she is now.

(LEAG, Higher Level, June 1988)

6 A French teacher in your school has written to a French friend hoping to arrange summer work for you and another pupil. Below is the reply which the teacher passes on to you. Write a letter in French to the French lady. You should write about 200 words.

Aigueblanche, le 2 mai

Cher Monsieur,

Je vous prie de m'excuser pour ma négligence à répondre si tard à vos deux lettres. Je vous réponds quant à la proposition concernant vos élèves qui souhaitent venir nous aider dans la ferme pendant l'été de 1988. Je serai bien heureuse de recevoir ces deux jeunes personnes. Vous m'avez dit qu'ils ont travaillé tous les deux en France l'année dernière. Il faut que les élèves m'écrivent pour me dire ce qu'ils ont fait exactement, c'est-à-dire, où ils ont travaillé, pendant combien de temps, quelle sorte de travail, ce qu'ils ont aimé et ce qui ne leur a pas plu. Aussi je voudrais savoir comment ils espèrent passer leurs vacances cette année s'ils viennent à notre ferme dans cette région montagneuse. Peut-être qu'ils ont des questions à me poser.

Ma fille Marie va chez sa correspondante en Allemagne au mois de juillet et Martin, mon fils, s'est cassé la jambe et s'est fait mal au dos dans un accident la semaine dernière. Donc j'ai grand besoin de ces élèves pour nous aider en juillet.

Recevez, Monsieur, mes très cordiales salutations.

Josette

(Northern Ireland Schools Examinations Council, Higher Level, June 1988)

7 You hope to spend a camping holiday in France with your family or with some friends, and have been given the address of a camp site. Write a letter in French in which you cover the points listed below. The address to which you should write is:

Camping 'La Castillanderie',
24290 Montignac-sur-Vézère,
Dordogne,
France.

Give the following information:
Dates of your stay – number of people in your group – how you are travelling – whether or not you are bringing your own tent.
Enquire about the following things:
Facilities on the site (e.g. showers, shop, restaurant, café, swimming pool etc.) – possibilities for sports etc. nearby – how far the site is from the nearest town.

Ask about the following things:
Price per night – booking in advance – deposit – directions for finding the site – time at which you should arrive.

End your letter appropriately

(Welsh Joint Education Committee, Higher Level, June 1988)

The following letter contains several numbered spaces. Using the list below the letter write out in French the words which would apply to your own circumstances.

Londres, ...(1)...............................

Monsieur,

Je voudrais passer ....(2)........................ avec ....(3)..............................
dans votre hôtel.

Pouvez-vous me réserver une chambre ....(4)..
avec douche et une chambre à deux personnes avec ....(5)..............................
pour les nuits ....(6)...
Est-ce qu'il y a ....(7).. dans toutes les
chambres? Nous préférons être au ....(8)..............................

Je voudrais savoir aussi s'il est possible de ....(9)...............................
à l'hôtel, et si l'hôtel se trouve ....(10).......................................
....

Je vous prie d'agréer, Monsieur, mes sentiments distingués.

.... (Signature)

Answers

(1) (today's date) ....

(2) (how long?) ....

(3) (who is accompanying you?) ....

(4) (what kind of room?) ....

(5) (washing facilities) ....

(6) (dates?) ....

(7) (some extra facility) ....

(8) (which floor?) ....

(9) (eating arrangements) ....

(10) (situation?) ....

(LEAG, Basic Level, June 1988)

9 Imagine you have just returned home from a family holiday in Brittany, where you spent a fortnight living in a small cottage (= un gîte), of which a description is given below. Write a letter telling a French friend about your holiday – where you went, for how long, what it was like, what you did, etc. Write about 100 words.

2 kms from the small village of le Gorvello (Morbihan), 15 kms E of Vannes and 19 kms from the sea. Tennis on the spot.

This attractive little gîte is situated in peaceful countryside on a small farm (mostly sheep and cows) in a slightly elevated position amongst pastures and woodland. A feature is the lovely large garden and, in particular, the recreational facilities which make the property so suitable for families: tennis, table tennis and pétanque are all available, although shared with French occupants of two other gîtes. Attached to the farmhouse of the owner and his family, some of whom speak English, our property is a stone building refurbished to provide modern, comfortable accommodation with a certain period character.

Kitchen/dining-room, sitting-room, 2 bedrooms with 1 double bed and 2 singles, shower-room, w.c., central heating (bedlinen included in prices).

(Sleeps 4)

(SEG, Extended Level, June 1988)

10 You have recently moved home. You are writing to a French pen-friend and you are telling him or her all about the new house or flat you have just moved into. Tell your friend about where you are living now. Here are some ideas for things you might include in your letter: the number of bedrooms, the number of rooms, how far away you are from the town-centre or nearest town, if you have a garden, a garage, and so on.

Try to keep your letter down to 50-70 words.

(Welsh Joint Education Committee, Basic Level, June 1988)

1 Write a letter in French, of 70/80 words, to the Syndicat d'Initiative at Dinard, including the points below:

(a) Give the dates when you will be at Dinard with your family.

(b) Say you would like some information about the town.

(c) Ask for a town plan and some brochures.

(d) Ask if you can also have a list of comfortable hotels which are near the sea and which are not expensive.

(e) Find out if there are some beaches where you can swim, and if there is a swimming pool.

Remember to start, date and end the letter in a suitable manner.

(SEG, General and Extended Level, June 1988)

Le

Syndicat
d'Initiative

de

DINARD

———

2, boulevard FÉART
TÉL. (99) 46.94.12

———

est à votre

disposition

pour tous

Renseignements

---

2 Write a letter in French of 60-70 words to your penfriend, inviting him/her to spend a fortnight with you. Make sure you include at least four of the points listed below, including one out of the last two.

Suggested dates – the best way to get to your town or village – information about your family – about your home.

What you might expect to do (e.g. swimming, walking) – visits you might make.

(LEAG, Basic Level, June 1988)

13 You receive a letter from your French friend, part of which appears below.

..... et nous comptons partir. dans les Pyrénées à Noël pour faire du ski. Nous avons pensé à toi. Est-ce que tu pourrais nous y accompagner? Si cela te plaît, demande tout de suite la permission à tes parents, puis écris-nous et dis-nous quand tu seras libre.

Est-ce que tu as déjà fait des sports d'hiver? As-tu fait du ski? Tu as des skis à toi? Si non, cela ne fait rien.

As-tu beaucoup de vêtements chauds? Si tu as des questions, pose-les.

Je joins des photos que nous avons prises. l'an dernier.

You ask your parents and they approve, subject to cost, so you write an immediate reply to your friend giving all the information asked for in this letter and asking questions about:
(i) cost
(ii) accommodation
(iii) length of stay

(Midland Examining Group, Higher Level, June 1988)

C000002996

Durham
MURDERS &
MISDEMEANOURS

John Van der Kiste

AMBERLEY

First published 2009

Amberley Publishing Plc
Cirencester Road, Chalford,
Stroud, Gloucestershire, GL6 8PE

www.amberleybooks.com

British Library Cataloguing in Publication Data.
A catalogue record for this book is available from the British Library.

ISBN 978 1 84868 149 1
Typesetting and Origination by Amberley Publishing
Printed in Great Britain

CONTENTS

INTRODUCTION

I was originally drawn to a study of murders in Durham during the 1870s after reading about Mary Ann Cotton, 'the West Auckland poisoner' according to the newspapers of her day, who was probably Britain's most prolific serial killer until Dr Harold Shipman was convicted over a century later. (Coincidentally, Shipman also served part of his sentence in Durham Gaol.) As is often the case, one piece of research led to another, until I was fascinated to discover how many other violent deaths there had been in the county that same decade. There were the inevitable domestic quarrels, aggravated by bad temper and alcohol (usually both together); there were cases of severe depression and attempted suicide, sometimes successful, sometimes not; there were scores to settle within the expatriate Irish community, occasionally with fatal results; and, as is sadly often the case, there was at least one instance where the perpetrator was too feeble-minded to appreciate the consequences of his actions. Add various misdemeanours of a lesser but still severe nature and the result is a considerable catalogue of crime in several varied forms.

In the contemporary press, there is sometimes considerable variation in the names of the main protagonists. Michael Gillingham, Gillighan and Gilligan (Darlington, 1875) are evidently one and the same person, as is, in an example of no mere difference of spelling, but also of name, William Gallon and William Bagnall (South Wingate, 1878). For such instances I have sometimes had to make an arbitrary decision for no particular reason.

My thanks go to my wife Kim for her tireless support and encouragement, and for reading through the draft; to my editors Sarah Flight and Jessica Andrews and designer James Pople for their help in seeing the book through to print; and to Paul Head, Harry Wynne, John Green, Simon Dell, Oliver Dixon and Gateshead Libraries & Arts Service, for the supply of photographs and general assistance. Every effort has been made to obtain permission to reuse material which may be in copyright, and I would be grateful if any holders of relevant material whose rights may have been inadvertently infringed would notify us, so that a suitable correction can be made to subsequent editions.

CHAPTER 1

NATURAL CAUSES OR MURDER?

Darlington, 1870

William Smith, who lived at Cobden Street, Eastbourne, Darlington, formerly worked as a clerk with Messrs Backhouse & Co., a local banking firm. He and his wife Elizabeth had three young children, the eldest a girl of seven. By the time he reached his thirties he suffered from perpetual ill health. In March 1870 he was dismissed by his employers. Time hung heavily on his hands, and relations between him and Elizabeth soon deteriorated.

Shortly before 7 a.m. on 20 March one of their neighbours, Jane Greenwood, was woken by a loud knock on the door. It was the Smiths' elder daughter saying that her mother wanted to see her urgently. Mrs Greenwood went next door and found Mrs Smith, fully dressed, in the passage, but the latter did not say a word to her. A puzzled Mrs Greenwood noticed the parlour door was open, looked into the room, and followed a still silent Mrs Smith inside. There, leaning against the cupboard door with his left arm resting on the floor, was the lifeless body of Mr Smith, his face, beard and hands covered in blood. The neighbour noticed a broken candlestick and walking stick lying beside him, the latter covered with blood and hair.

As Elizabeth Smith was clearly in an uncommunicative frame of mind, and probably suffering from shock, Mrs Greenwood left the house without saying a word. She had not heard any noise from next door during the night, and although it must have taken little imagination to work out what had happened, she refrained from jumping to conclusions.

On returning to her house she asked her husband James to go in to see for himself. After he had done so he called Dr Edward Jackson and Sergeant John Lynn, who both arrived within a few minutes. The latter spoke to the Greenwoods, saw the body and a large amount of blood around the house, noticed a walking stick with blood and hair, and a broken candlestick both lying around. He accordingly charged Mrs Smith with killing her husband. 'It was all his own fault, it was not mine,' she said, 'he has done nothing but drink lately, and tumble about.' As the sergeant took an uncorked bottle containing a small amount of whisky from the deceased's pocket, and a tumbler glass from his left breast pocket, he realised that the dead man's intemperate habits must have obviously played a large part in the case.

On the next day, the Smiths' cleaner Christiana Swainston came to work at the house and noticed a shawl lying around, but did not see anything unusual about it. Later it was handed to her to wash, by which time it had a large quantity of blood on it, and she had to soak it for a while before the blood would come out.

An inquest was held on 22 March at Darlington Police Court under Mr Dean, the deputy coroner. All those taking part assembled at the court at 9.45 a.m., then went to Eastbourne to see the body of Mr Smith before returning to court where proceedings began. Mrs Greenwood, who had lived next door to the Smiths for less than a month, described their daughter's visit on Sunday morning, going to the house and seeing Mr Smith lying dead. They had both been in her house on the Thursday evening, and both seemed 'very peaceable'. Even so, she knew that it had not always been thus. On another night that week she had heard Mrs Smith screaming and went into the house to find a very distressed, sober wife and a very drunken husband.

This was corroborated by her husband James who had followed his wife in on Sunday morning, seen Mr Smith's body and remarked that this was 'a very sad affair'. Mrs Smith, he said, did not reply, but held her hands over her face as if she were crying. He invited her to go into their house, but she still did not respond. On the Wednesday evening when she had been screaming, he went into the house and heard Mr Smith using 'very violent language' against his wife.

To counteract this picture of a perpetual drunk, Francis Thompson, a Darlington cabman, said he had taken Mr Smith on 19 March, shortly after 3 p.m., to cash a cheque at the bank, and then to the Bull's Head, where he got him a glass of whisky and a bottle of soda water. After he had drunk half the whisky, Thompson drove him home, and he still seemed reasonably sober.

Edward Jackson, the surgeon, described entering the house — where he immediately saw a great deal of blood — and finding the body lying against the cupboard. He said he thought Mr Smith had been killed in another room and the body moved several hours later. The door was only slightly smeared, and there was just a three-inch trickle of blood on the door behind him. There would have been much more than that if the fatal injuries had been inflicted there. The head was covered with blood, and three straight wounds below, two about three inches apart, running in a parallel direction, with the third in a transverse direction, had presumably been caused by some blunt instrument. He did not think they were the result of a fall, as they were on the top of his head. They had presumably happened when he was attacked with the stick, covered with brown hair and blood, lying near the window of the front room. On the back of the left forearm were several bruises which might also have been produced by the stick. The back of the hand and the back of the left-hand fingers were bruised, probably through the deceased having tried to shield his head, while the walls marked with blood had been rubbed, as if a clumsy attempt had been made to rub out the stains, while there were two pieces of wallpaper and two umbrellas lying in the blood. There was no indication that any struggle had taken place.

A Durham County policeman in uniform,
c. 1880 (© John C. Green)

On going into the kitchen and examining the passage, he saw a drop of blood on the front doormat, about a foot from the parlour door. If the deceased had walked along the passage after being wounded, he would have seen much more. He thought Smith had been attacked in that part of the parlour where the most blood was found, and there was no question of his wounds being self-inflicted.

After statements from Dr Arrowsmith and Sergeant Lynn, Mr Nixon, who was representing the prisoner, said there was no firm evidence that Mr Smith's wounds had been inflicted by the violence of another person. Nevertheless the jury only retired for fifteen minutes before returning with a verdict that the deceased had been murdered by the prisoner. She had been sitting in an adjoining room and was brought in to hear the verdict, which she received impassively.

Another hearing took place on 24 March at the borough police court before the magistrates. Most of the same witnesses were called a second time. In addition to her previous testimony, Mrs Greenwood said that on the Wednesday night she had seen Mr Smith put out his hand and try to strike his wife as she lay on the bed. Further evidence of the abusive relationship was provided by another neighbour, Mrs Burlison. After telling the police that Mrs Smith only drank spirits 'when she could get any', a statement greeted with much laughter in court, and saying she only drank beer, she said that Mr Smith was dangerous when drunk and on occasion she had had to protect the wife. He once threatened to run her through with a sword.

In summing up Mr Nixon said that if the bench thought there was any evidence on which to commit the accused, it should be for manslaughter rather than murder. When the clerk to the magistrates charged her, she declared that she was innocent. She was remanded in custody, and on 14 July she was charged at Durham Assizes Crown Court before Mr Justice Lush, charged with manslaughter. Mr Skidmore and Mr Edge were counsel for the prosecution, and Campbell Foster and Mr Meynell for the defence.

Mrs Greenwood, called as the first witness, described the events of that fatal morning. Under cross-examination on the subject of Mr Smith's drinking, she said she was not in a position to know whether the reason for his discharge from the bank was connected with his drinking habits.

Her husband James, corroborating her evidence, spoke of seeing inside the house and noticing bloodstains on the right-hand side of the passage wall, between the parlour and kitchen doors and near the stairs. Both marks looked as if somebody had put his hand out to steady himself. Mrs Smith said nothing to him about her husband having tumbled downstairs at about 2 a.m. He looked carefully both at the front and back of the house, but could not find any marks of blood or of anybody having fallen.

Dr Jackson also repeated his evidence given earlier and reported on the post-mortem, in which he was assisted by Dr Page and Dr Harrow Smith. A haemorrhage from wounds in the head, he said, would have made Smith lose consciousness and bleed to death, although it would have been simple enough for anyone to have stopped the bleeding. There were some fresh-looking bruises on the outer part of the left thigh, on both ankles and older ones on the bridge of the nose and above his right eyebrow. On removing the scalp he found the wounds did not go down to the bone, and there was a considerable effusion of blood beneath and around the wounds. He could not determine whether the deceased was intoxicated at the time of his death.

On being cross-examined by Mr Foster, he said he never heard of a scalp wound continuing to bleed until a person bled to death. If Smith had fallen, it was reasonable to suppose that he would make some effort to get to his feet as long as he was still conscious. Three yards was not too far for a man already on his feet to lurch if he suddenly felt faint. He did not think that blood on the wall was the result of a man falling with his head against the wall. The deceased's kidneys were congested, his liver was enlarged, presumably through drinking, and was therefore liable to bleed more than that of a healthy person. He did not think the deceased's skin would be more liable than usual to fracture.

After similar medical evidence from Dr Arrowsmith the next witness was Annie Hart, a former live-in servant with the Smiths for two years who had left them about a fortnight before his death. The shirt produced belonged to Mrs Smith, and she last saw her wearing it on the day she left her service. It had the candle marks on it, but not the bloodstains.

Mrs Swainston testified to having seen the shawl without blood on the Monday and washing the same bloodstained garment two days later. When cross-examined by Mr Foster she said she had asked Mrs Smith whether she should wash it and was told she could, as it would not be 'wanted' (presumably as evidence in court).

For the defence, Robert Hopkins, a clerk with Backhouse & Co., said he had known Mr Smith for about four years, and his drink problem was common knowledge. He remembered Smith having had an attack of dizziness about eighteen months earlier, and apparently cured him on the spot with the aid of some brandy. Shortly afterwards he had a similar attack, and he was discharged from the firm about a fortnight before his death. Whether it was on the grounds of his heavy drinking, the witness was reluctant to comment.

Having heard all the medical evidence, Dr Donkin, a Newcastle surgeon, and lecturer in Medical Jurisprudence at Durham University, said he did not think the wounds on the head were particularly dangerous, and doubted if they would have been enough to cause insensibility. They seemed perfectly consistent with a man being seized with a fainting fit while walking, and falling on the ground. Death from fatty degeneration of the heart or syncope would leave the heart empty, and cause the pale condition of the brain referred to by Mr Jackson. The effusion of serum on the brain would certainly produce giddiness and cause a man to fall, and any additional mildly life-threatening conditions would probably kill a man in such circumstances.

When questioned by the judge, he said the wounds were not enough to produce the fatal syncope, which came about from natural causes. Contact with any hard substance could have accounted for the bruising on the arms. He did not believe that haemorrhage was the cause of death; it was more probably a result of disease of the brain and the heart, exacerbated by his intemperate habits. Under Mr Skidmore's cross-examination, he said a more careful examination would be necessary to confirm the theory that death had been produced by haemorrhage. In response to further questioning by the judge, he said he would not like to suggest that death was accelerated by the wounds, although it was possible.

'I really must have a positive answer,' the judge insisted.

Dr Donkin then said he thought the violence probably would have hastened Mr Smith's demise. Feeling they were on the point of moving too far away from the main issue, the judge reminded them that the real point was not 'the approximate cause of death' but whether death was 'accelerated by the wounds'. Another witness, Dr Jobson of Bishop Auckland, said the medical evidence was consistent with the theory that the cause of death was heart disease.

In summing up, Mr Justice Lush said the jury would not have to take the medical part of the question into consideration, as the doctors called by the defence had admitted that death had been hastened by the wounds. They had to decide whether death resulted from a fall from faintness, either inside or outside the house, or from blows inflicted by his wife.

The jury retired for half an hour and then returned a verdict of 'guilty', with a recommendation to mercy. When the judge asked, 'on what ground?' the foreman said it was on account of provocation Mrs Smith may have received from her husband.

As he passed sentence, the judge said he entirely concurred in the jury's verdict. The prisoner had been guilty of a crime little short of murder, and she was fortunate not to have been committed for trial on such a charge. Making every allowance for the jury's recommendation, under the circumstances he felt he could not pass a less severe sentence than ten years' penal servitude.

When she was removed from the dock, Mrs Smith looked as if she was about to faint.

CHAPTER 2

THE CRUELTY OF JANE ARMSTRONG

Hendon, Sunderland, 1870-71

In September 1870, Mr Crocker of Newcastle saw a house advertised for sale at Mainsforth Terrace, Hendon, Sunderland. When he came to view, he spoke to one of the residents, Jane Armstrong, who lived at No. 60 in the same road. In the course of conversation with him, she mentioned casually that she had 'a poor creature in her house' whom she often had to chain up and tie to the bedpost as she was so badly behaved and used to destroy her clothes. After he had left, a suspicious Mr Crocker passed the information to the Mayor of Sunderland and the borough magistrates. They had already heard reports of strange noises coming from an upstairs room, and as the house was not licensed as an asylum, the police and authorities would need to investigate.

On the morning of 12 September two officers, Detective Peacock and Constable Brown, went to pay the premises a visit. When Mrs Armstrong opened the front door, Peacock told her that neighbours had expressed concerns about cries and other noises from the house and asked if he could see the woman upstairs. At first she refused to let him in, then she changed her mind and told him that if he would come back in a couple of hours' time he could see her then. He said he would not leave, but would only wait for another fifteen minutes. If she did not cooperate within this time, he would take legal action against her.

Realising she had no alternative, Mrs Armstrong went upstairs and soon reappeared, accompanied by a thinly clad woman of haggard appearance. (Another account says that the woman was not brought downstairs by Mrs Armstrong, and the officer did not discover her until he was shown upstairs, opened the door to the room and saw her chained to an iron bedstead). When Peacock questioned the other woman, she answered that she had been confined and chained up in bed, and when taken out into the open air, the shock of fresh air and sunlight made her dizzy. He then told Mrs Armstrong that he needed to see the room in which the woman had been kept.

With reluctance she led him upstairs. As he entered the darkened room, he was hit by such an appalling stench that he had to step out again at once. After bracing himself in the name of duty, he investigated further. The only light came from a crack in the window board, nailed against the window, but it was enough for him to notice that the contents of the room

*'Cruelty to a lunatic at Sunderland', a drawing of September 1870 showing Jane Armstrong ill-treating Mary Ann Hobson. According to Mrs Armstrong's subsequent letter to the papers, allegations of ill-treatment were unfounded (*Illustrated Police News*)*

comprised a narrow iron bedstead and a square broken box, which the woman had been given to place her dinner on. There was a pallet and dirty pot for a lavatory, but no chair, table or washstand, and pieces of rope were strewn around the floor. The woman in question, Mary Ann Hobson, had apparently been confined in this room for nine years, virtually a prisoner. A warrant was obtained for her removal, and she was taken to the union workhouse.

Peacock questioned Mrs Hobson, a widow of about sixty-five, and she said she had become very ill after her husband died. Another relative had left her an annuity of a guinea per week, hoping this would be enough to enable her to live in comfort for the rest of her life. When Mrs Armstrong learnt of this, she offered to let her come and stay in her own home so she could look after her. However, Mrs Hobson's mental health soon deteriorated and she became increasingly confused. It had been easy for Mrs Armstrong to persuade her solicitors, by fair means or foul, to sign a document allowing her as *de facto* guardian to collect the money on her behalf. Although Mrs Hobson might have been a simple-minded soul and somewhat confused, she was well aware that her so-called protector was spending the money on herself instead. Though increasingly frail, she tried to put up a fight, but Mrs Armstrong easily got the better of her and chained her to the bed, telling her she would only be set free when she calmed down and learned to behave herself.

A policeman on the beat at Sunderland
© Paul Head

When reports appeared in the press, Mrs Armstrong was not unnaturally anxious to defend herself. If she is to be believed, several statements were patently untrue. She said that the police did not find any chains in the room, and the surgeon who examined Mrs Hobson found no evidence of ill usage. Likewise the woman was not thinly clad or haggard but remarkably well. The rope referred to on the floor was a clothesline, which she had taken down that morning and left on the stairhead. She had objected to the police officers seeing Mrs Hobson immediately, as she was still in bed and it was only reasonable to wait until she had had a chance to dress. Finally, she could not have been confined in the room for nine years, as the house had only been built three years ago.

Even so, some of the charges could not be denied. On 11 October Mrs Armstrong appeared before the magistrates at Sunderland on a charge of unlawfully receiving into her house and taking charge of a lunatic for profit, and without first having an order and medical certificate, as required by the Act for regulating the care and treatment of lunatics. To these charges were added the fact that her house was not licensed for the reception of lunatics and was not a registered hospital or asylum, and above all that she had abused and ill treated Mary Ann Hobson for a number of years.

It was established that at first the latter had received the money herself, until Mrs Armstrong's chicanery ensured that it went into her pocket after that. Once the magistrates had received a full report of the conditions in which Mrs Hobson was held, Mrs Armstrong appeared in court a second time on 11 October. Witnesses were called to give evidence against her and she was committed for trial at the next Durham Spring Assizes.

The case was heard before Baron Martin on 2 March 1871. Mr Quain and Mr Abbs appeared for the prosecution, representing the Commissioners in Lunacy, and there was no counsel for the defence. Two witnesses testified to having paid a yearly annuity to Mrs Armstrong for the maintenance of Mrs Hobson, one from 1860 to 1864, and the other since 1864.

While Mrs Armstrong could hardly plead her innocence with regard to her house being unlicensed, she protested that she was not guilty of any charge of cruelty. Mrs Hobson, she insisted, was violent and dangerous, and had to be kept under restraint for her own good. After retiring for a short time, the jury found the prisoner guilty only on the first count, of keeping a lunatic without being licensed, although they accepted that there was not sufficient proof of cruelty. She was sentenced to three months' imprisonment.

CHAPTER 3

THE SPENNYMOOR SHOP MURDER

Spennymoor, 1872

On the evening of Saturday 16 November 1872, thirty-nine-year-old Joseph and Jane Waine were sitting in the back kitchen of their house adjoining their shop at Duncombe Street, Spennymoor. With them were their lodger John Wilson, an Irishman, and the Waines' eleven-year-old son, Isaac. While they were in the back kitchen of their house behind the shop, Hugh Slane, one of their regular customers, came in by the back door and asked for a halfpenny box of matches.

As Mrs Waine went to fetch one from the shop for him, Slane turned to Wilson, asking, 'Are you the man that was in Carrick's public house tonight?' Wilson said he was not, as he was a stranger in the town; he did not have the money to go to Carrick's, and did not even know where the pub was. When Slane told him angrily that he was a liar, Waine came to Wilson's defence. 'Don't impose upon a stranger,' he said, 'take my word, Slane, he has not been out tonight.' Slane went out of the back door into the yard, inviting Waine to follow him. Wilson and Mrs Waine both took this as a challenge to go out and fight, and persuaded him to stay where he was.

Furious at being thwarted, Slane came back indoors and thrust the box of matches in his face, then went out again. Waine lit his pipe and stood leaning against his front door. Slane had gone from the back yard by the passage into the street, then came round to the door at the front, seized Waine by the collar of his coat, dragged him halfway up the passage and gave a loud whistle. Next he tripped Waine up by putting his leg between Waine's and held him down across the passage on his back by the collar and the throat.

Isaac Waine ran out after his father and tried to help him but was knocked down and fell against his father's prostrate form. Immediately after hearing the whistle three friends, John Hays, Terence Rice and George Beesley, all ran from Hays' house nearby into the passage. Slane was stooping over Waine and holding him down by the neck, saying threateningly, 'If I get a kick at him it will be his last'. Hays then told Rice and Beesley to stand to each side of the passage while he gave Waine a running kick twice in the side. Slane, Rice and Beesley all took turns in kicking the shopkeeper as well. Isaac was kicked in the head, although he was not badly hurt.

Cheapside, Spennymoor, early twentieth century

High Street, Spennymoor, early twentieth century

Mrs Waine ran into the passage and tried to pull Rice away from her husband. Hays seized her by the head and pulled her out of the passage, pulling her cap and shawl off, but she ran back again and saw Hays take a running kick at her husband. The intruders then left, and the lodger Wilson went into the passage so he could help Waine back on his feet. Badly weakened by the assault, Waine could not walk without supporting himself against the wall. He made his way painfully into the house, crying out feebly, 'I'm done, I'm done.'

Dr O'Hanlon and an assistant were called to examine him and found him vomiting. They prescribed him some medicine and helped him take it, but within twenty minutes he was dead. A post-mortem showed that all the internal organs were healthy, and the cause of death could only be attributed to the violent attack. Kicks on the stomach with heavy hob-nailed boots such as the men had been wearing were likely to produce a nervous shock which often proved fatal.

Bondgate Police Station, Bishop Auckland © Paul Head

Mrs Waine had known Slane and Hays for some time, and she knew the others by sight. She and her son were able to identify them all. An inquest was held at the police court in Bishop Auckland on 22 November, adjourned to allow time for additional evidence and reconvened a couple of days later. Superintendent Henderson conducted evidence on behalf of the police, and the prisoners were represented by Mr Hutchinson. The coroner, Mr Trotter, alleged that Waine had come by his death 'through some club or faction combination'. It emerged that Waine had refused to attend a Fenian amnesty demonstration in the town about a fortnight earlier. In view of the intense local feeling and general fury against those responsible for the brutal killing of a very popular member of the community, it had been thought advisable for the prisoners to be removed in irons under a strong police escort to Bishop Auckland.

Waine's son Isaac said he saw Hugh Slane drag his father into the passage, then whistle loudly as a prearranged signal for the other men to appear. This, said Mr Trotter in summing up, was surely enough to dispel any doubt that the prisoners' attack, if not the killing, was premeditated, and the jury returned a verdict of wilful murder. At the same time Mrs Hays was charged with threatening Mrs Waine at her husband's funeral and sentenced to one month in prison in default of finding sureties for her good behaviour.

The case came to trial at Durham Assizes on 17 December before Mr Justice Denman, with Mr Trotter and Mr Edge for the prosecution, Mr Blackwell for the defence. The prosecution could not find Wilson, who had refused to give evidence before the coroner, left town and could not be traced. Nevertheless the basic facts were beyond dispute. During the first part of the proceedings some time was lost in trying to get an accurate description of the locality from the evidence of a policeman, as there was no map of the shop, house and surrounding area available and no legal obligation on the part of the Crown to have one drawn specially for the purpose. The waste of time caused by this examination, it was estimated, probably cost three or four times as much as any map would have done. It then transpired that the counsel for the prosecution had had no consultation to advise as to this and other matters before the trial, as again the Crown did not permit such expense. The judge called it 'scandalous and disgraceful' to the Treasury and to the county to imperil a prosecution like this for want of necessary means.

As far as some of the prisoners were concerned, said the defence, their participation in the violence was not satisfactorily proved. There was no evidence of premeditation or intent to murder the deceased, the testimony of the widow and her son was in many respects conflicting, and the passage was so dark that they could easily have been mistaken when it came to identifying Mr Waine's assailants.

It was left to the judge to remind the jury that if these men were acting together with the unlawful purpose of merely giving the deceased a sound beating, but then brought about his death by their violence, it was murder. If they could see anything in the evidence which would exculpate any of the prisoners, they ought to acquit them, or if there was anything which they thought could have provoked the violence, such as a previous quarrel or blows given by the deceased, they might then find the prisoners guilty of manslaughter, but he was unable to point out any such evidence. He commented in severe terms on the time that had been wasted for want of a plan, in trying to get a description of the place from a policeman. It might have rendered it necessary to adjourn the case, at great expense, to the following day, and he also spoke of 'the imperfect way' in which some of the evidence had been placed before them for want of a previous consultation of counsel. Was it not disgraceful and scandalous, he asked, for a paltry saving of three or four guineas to risk the failure of a prosecution in this way? Although he stressed it was his own opinion, he was sure that other judges would agree.

The jury retired for about forty-five minutes and returned with a verdict of 'guilty' against all four prisoners. The judge pronounced sentence of death on thirty-two-year-old Slane, nineteen-year-old Rice, twenty-nine-year-old Hays and twenty-seven-year-old Beesley, saying they had been found guilty of a brutal murder on the clearest evidence and it was clear that it was their intention when they entered Waine's house either to kill him or the lodger Wilson.

> You deliberately kicked to death a fellow-creature; and if it be held that this was anything but the offence of murder, it would be turning the whole world into a wilderness of misery and crime, and preventing any peace or happiness from remaining on the face of the earth. I won't attempt to aggravate your miserable feelings, for I'm sure they must be miserable at this moment, at having to receive sentence of death which I must pass upon you.

All the prisoners received their sentence with apparent indifference and expressed their determination to die like men.

Petitions were launched locally in order to try and spare the lives of at least two of the prisoners. According to the press, they met with little support; 'the news of a respite would be received with deep dissatisfaction, it is not very likely that many will petition for any extension of mercy to those who showed none to poor Waine.' The Howard Association wrote to H. Austin Bruce, the Home Secretary, and on 4 January an official from Whitehall replied that the Secretary felt warranted in commuting the capital sentence in the case of Rice and Beesley to penal servitude for life, but could find no grounds for doing likewise with Hays and Slane.

The *Newcastle Courant* took issue with the granting of reprieves:

The deed was one of the most brutal which has been committed for a long time; the men, with one exception, perhaps, were as clearly guilty as evidence could prove them; and Durham, which has been the scene of so many outrages, just required such an example as a quadruple execution would have been to cow its lawless spirits into subjection, to let them see that policemen were not made to be kicked, that women were not sent into the world to be the victims of their brutal passions, and that knife-drawing, pistol-shooting vagabonds would not be allowed to take or endanger the lives of peaceful citizens with impunity. Unfortunately for the peace of our neighbouring county, Mr Bruce has, however, foolishly allowed himself to be swayed by the common, but most irrational prejudice against hanging several men for one crime, and has respited two of the convicted murderers. Had he extended the clemency to Beesley alone, whose actual participation in the deed is not demonstrated, by evidence so overpowering as that which proves the guilt of his companions, the public would have probably acquiesced in the decision...

During their imprisonment the men were attended by Canon Consett, of the Roman Catholic Church, who administered to them the last sacrament on the morning of Sunday 10 January 1873. He asked for the prayers of the Catholic congregation on behalf of the condemned men at morning service, stating that they were prepared to die.

Calcraft had arrived in Durham on Saturday 9 January, four days before the executions took place. Hays said he was very pleased to see reporters present, and he was happy to die. He stood there innocent of the murder of Joseph Waine, having seen him at midday on the Saturday that he died — and that, he maintained, was the last time. While there he took the opportunity to thank the governor, deputy governor and all around him for their kindness, the minister and his flock for having prayed for him. He also thanked God he was leaving this world for a better one. As he was innocent, it was hard for him to leave his wife and children. He asked the Lord to have mercy on his soul and to have mercy upon and bless Father Consett. While speaking he wept a good deal, and as he could not lift his hands because they were pinioned, he asked for somebody to come and wipe away his tears.

'Thank God, I am dying innocent,' he said. 'I am happy; I am going to a better world. I am sure that the other three boys are as innocent as me. If Slane did it, it was before he came into my house; but he is as innocent as a child in its mother's womb. May the Lord forgive the woman who swore my life away. It is hard to see a man cut down in life innocent, and leave a wife and three children with nobody to care for them.'

A procession was formed, consisting of the Sheriff first, then Slane and a priest, followed by Hays and another priest. Both men of the cloth accompanied the condemned man to the scaffold, and remained until all was over. As Hays could not write, just before his execution he left a statement which he had dictated and signed with his mark:

I believe I am going to die for the perjury of the woman that lived with Waine and her son and Sergeant Scott, for swearing that we were all Fenians — that is more than I knew. I always loved a working man. I always did help them when they were hungry or dry. The jury found us guilty and passed sentence of death upon us. It is not for the death of Joseph Waine altogether that we are going to be hung. It is just the report that has been in the press. It went about the country that we were outraged Fenians. That is the very thing we are going to be hung for this morning...

Mrs Waine had not been the only person to connect him with Irish nationalist sympathies. According to the *Middlesborough Gazette*, Hays and his wife had lived in Stockton about three or four years previously, and he was known there as the 'Tipperary Cock', an outspoken Fenian sympathiser whose house was a general rendezvous for 'suspected characters'. Though not considered particularly brave, he had a remarkable facility for being present at many a disturbance, and often appeared at the police courts afterwards. He never seemed to have any money on him when he was fined, but somebody always paid his fines promptly. On one occasion he sustained a slight cut on his head, and sent for the doctor. When the latter examined the cut, Hays 'alarmed the whole neighbourhood by bellowing out as though his head was going to be cut off'.

The Hays family had to leave Stockton in a hurry one day, and when the next tenant of the house moved in, he found a loose floorboard. On looking underneath he found a revolver, several old swords and some pikes, evidently put there in reserve for some demonstration. There can have been few people in authority in Durham who were not relieved to see the passing of such a troublesome character.

CHAPTER 4

'MURDER GREW WITH HER'

West Auckland, 1872

'Poisoning — the most secret means of murder — has been most successful in the hands of women,' the *Northern Echo* of 10 March 1873 told its readers. It was reporting on the conviction earlier that week of Mary Ann Cotton, of whom it wrote that 'her successes are almost unparalleled in the history of crime'. There is no certainty as to exactly how many people she killed, but as many as twenty or more may have met death at her hands. Having eluded detection for many years, she achieved the dubious distinction of being almost certainly the nation's most prolific serial killer.

Mary Ann Robson was born at Low Moorsley, on or around 12 October 1832. Her parents, Michael, a miner, and Mary, *née* Lonsdale, were both probably in their late teens at the time. There were three children in all, the two younger being Margaret, born in 1834, and Robert, a year later. The former, not recorded in the 1841 census, presumably died young. As a child Mary Ann was said to be pretty with dark hair and eyes. During adolescence she was a teacher at a Wesleyan Methodist Sunday school. Even so she was not necessarily a paragon of virtue, and it was rumoured (admittedly, possibly with hindsight) that as a child she had deliberately killed a boy by pushing him down a pit shaft.

Facts about the family's early life are often contradictory. According to different sources, her father died in 1842 or 1846, aged either twenty-six or thirty, after falling down a shaft while repairing a pulley wheel. Despite his daughter's subsequent history, there is no reason to doubt that his death was a genuine accident and nothing to do with her. His widow subsequently married George Stott, who lived at Seaton Colliery, and opened a village school in Murton.

Mary Ann left home at the age of sixteen and became a live-in nursemaid to the family of Edward Potter, a colliery manager at South Hetton, for three years, and then she went back to Murton to help her mother run the school. She was already pregnant when she married twenty-six-year-old William Mowbray, a labourer, on 18 July 1852, at Newcastle Register Office. They travelled around the country in search of work, making their first home either in Plymouth or Cornwall. Here she gave birth to four children, of whom all but one died, apparently from natural causes. They returned north to Hendon in 1856, where she had three more children, all but one of whom were dead within a year of their birth.

Mowbray took out life insurance policies on himself and the remaining children. He died in January 1865, a few hours after a violent attack of diarrhoea. It is thought that his wife may have helped him on his way with arsenic, as he was unable to work through ill health and their standard of living had deteriorated. She was said to have had 'a horror of poverty', and the insurance money of £35 gave her an incentive to kill him. If he did die of natural causes — and it is only fair to give her the benefit of the doubt — this may have inspired her to take out insurance on any future husbands she might (and did) have. Two of the children soon followed him to the grave, and she collected about £30 in insurance as a result.

Another theory suggests that, assuming she had lost her first few children by natural causes in an age of high infant mortality, she no longer found it easy to form any strong maternal bond with any of her subsequent children. Callous as it may sound, if they were expendable commodities whose premature deaths would result in another insurance payout then so be it.

On 28 August 1865 she married George Ward, an engineer, and they lived in Sunderland. After a bout of fever, Ward was too weak to work and soon the only money he was bringing into the household was parish relief of 4s a week. He fell ill with a mysterious wasting disease and died on 21 October 1866, aged thirty-three. It was thought that his wife resented the state of poverty to which his unemployment had reduced them, and the fact that they had no children suggested that it might not have been a happy marriage. Although the doctors attended him during his last illness, at the time no mention was made of the possibility that he might have been poisoned.

By Christmas 1866 the widowed Mary Ann Ward had become housekeeper to James Robinson, a shipwright whose wife Hannah had died in November that year, leaving him with five small children. Within a few days of going to work for him, she became his mistress. The youngest child, John, aged ten months, died on 4 January 1867 within less than a fortnight of her arrival, and the doctor who arrived after his death gave the cause as gastric fever.

At around this time she went to look after her mother, now Mrs Stott, saying to incredulous neighbours that she feared she would die before long. This was the first and by no means the last time she would 'predict' that one of her relatives did not have long to live. Mrs Stott died on 15 March 1867 at the age of fifty-four, about nine days after her daughter's arrival, and was buried at Old Seaham. This time there was no insurance money to be collected, but while she was at her mother's house Mary Ann helped herself to some of the clothing and bedding. She probably assumed she was entitled to it as part of her inheritance, but it angered her stepfather, who thought she was being insensitive and grasping to think of material gain at such a time. After she had left he said he would not allow her into the house again.

Little John Robinson, who had died at the beginning of the year, was the first of six children to be buried within the next twelve months. His brother, six-year-old James, followed him on 7 April and their eight-year-old sister Elizabeth six days later. Of Mary Ann's children by Mowbray, nine-year-old Elizabeth died on 26 April and Isabella on 2 May. All had very similar symptoms of foaming at the mouth, retching — especially after being given something to drink — and rolling around the bed in agony. The cause of death in each case was given as gastric fever, and they were buried at Bishopwearmouth Cemetery. Despite the disapproval of Robinson's three sisters, who suspected that the deaths of the children were not accidental, he married his mistress on 11 August 1867 at Bishopwearmouth church. Their daughter, Mary Isabella, was born on 29 November, christened at St Andrew's church, Pallion, on 18 February, died apparently of gastric fever a few days later and was buried on 1 March. In the burial register her name was given as Margaret.

By this time, Robinson was about to discover the scale of debts run up by his wife. He earned reasonable money and had made some savings, which he intended to put towards buying his own house. From her point of view, the fewer children they had, the more money there would be for him — or her. She had suggested he should have his life and the lives of his remaining children insured, but after he refused to consider the idea, she began to steal from his savings account. It seems that she was something of a spendthrift whose money went on little luxuries, particularly fine dresses, resented having little money to spend on herself, and any husband without money or the means of obtaining it was of no use to her.

Early in 1869, one of the Sunderland building societies checked his passbook and found that certain amounts paid in had been altered by the addition of strokes denoting an additional ten shillings — unofficial alterations made with obvious intent to defraud. A shocked Robinson defended his wife, insisting that she had paid in the amounts stated and it must be one of the society's clerks who was at fault. When the society threatened to take legal action against him, he had second thoughts, and ordered her to make the £5 worth of payments they were requesting. When she told him that the society did not want the accumulated payments for another week, he realised that she must be to blame.

A few days later, he found that she was trying to borrow £5 from a loan office, giving the names of his uncle and brother-in-law as guarantors. His son then told him that she had been sending him to the pawnbrokers to redeem some of his household linen and other goods. She also had charge of his bank book and his building society passbook, and when he checked it again, he found she had misappropriated at least £50 and entered sums in the building society book which she had never paid in.

Enough was enough, he decided, as he taxed her with dishonesty over their finances, and told her the rumours he had heard about the children's deaths. Horrified at being found out, she said she could obtain the £5 from her stepfather, but he would not hear of it. He told her they would have to separate, and in order to protect his good name it would be her responsibility to explain herself to the building societies in Sunderland. In order to discuss and resolve any outstanding business, he would meet her on Deptford Bridge later that day after he had finished working. After he had left the house she got dressed, took one of the children (whether a boy or girl is not known), about eighteen months old, went out, and abandoned it with friends. She told them she was going to post a letter, but she did not come back. The child was returned to him in a wretched state but, unlike so many of its siblings, at least it survived.

Robinson never spoke to her again and never saw any more of her apart from catching what he thought was a glimpse of her at chapel one Sunday evening. After she had gone, he was at last, in a position to uncover the full extent of his debts which she had incurred. He shut up his house and moved in with his married sister in Coronation Street, Sunderland.

Later he said he was convinced that all the children had been poisoned, and though he suspected so at the time, he did not like to dwell on such a subject. They had all been healthy and strong, and only fell ill a few days before they died. He noticed that they had always vomited after she gave them something to eat or drink. His sisters had often talked to him both then and since about the children's suspicious deaths. When they read about 'the West Auckland poisoning case' in the newspapers a few months later, they told him that this was the way his children went. One of them handed him a paper, saying, 'That is thy Mary Ann that has been doing that'. Only then did he realise that her efforts to take out insurance on his life and the surviving children were part of a sinister design.

Early in 1870 Margaret Cotton, who had known her for some years, introduced her to her brother Frederick. Neither of them were aware how many husbands she had had and lost rather quickly. Frederick Cotton, who worked at the Coronation pit, North Walbottle, where he lived, had just lost his wife Adelaide to consumption, and one of their four children to typhoid. A second child, Adelaide Jane, also succumbed to the same illness. He was left with two small sons, and Margaret had just moved in to help look after them. On 25 March 1870, after being taken ill with severe stomach pains, the previously healthy Margaret Cotton died, aged thirty-eight, leaving £60 in the bank. Mary Ann did her best to console him, and he married her as Mary Ann Mowbray on 17 September 1870 at St Andrew's church, Newcastle. At the time he was unaware that her legal name was Mary Ann Robinson and that the marriage was bigamous.

Mr and Mrs Cotton had not been at Walbottle long before she fell out with their neighbours, who accused her of poisoning their pigs, and they moved to Johnson Terrace, West Auckland. At this time the family consisted of herself, her husband Frederick, her nine-year-old stepson Frederick Cotton, seven-year-old stepson Charles Cotton, and their son of fourteen months Robert Cotton, born in January 1871. Later that year her husband, who had previously been healthy, was taken ill at work with severe gastric pains. After lingering at home for a few days he died on 19 September 1871, his age being variously given as thirty-three or thirty-nine, and his death was ascribed to gastric fever. Almost at once she received funds provided by sympathetic neighbours and free coal from local mine owners.

About three months after his death she took a lodger, Joseph Nattrass, a widower aged thirty-five, and he made a will in which she was the main beneficiary. On 9 March 1872 her ten-year-old stepson Frederick died, and the agent from the Prudential Insurance Office paid her £5 15s. Her fourteen-month-old son Robert followed his half-brother to the grave on 28 March, and she probably received a similar insurance payout again. As was the case with her last husband, both children were buried at the parish's expense. She still gave every appearance of being in dire poverty, and continued to receive relief from the parish. Nobody, she decided, needed to know about the insurance claims.

By now Nattrass, who was paying 11s per week for lodging and board, had become engaged to Mary Ann Cotton. He had always enjoyed the best of health, but now he became ill and thought he might be suffering from Bright's Disease. When a friend visited him, he said, 'If I was only better I will be out of this'. On 31 March he told a medical attendant, who was treating him for gastric fever, that he had no more fever than the doctor himself had. Had it not been for the grinding pain in his stomach he would have been all right, and he refused to take any more of the medicine prescribed for him. He died in agony on 1 April, leaving Mary Ann £10 and a watch. Her only encumbrance now was her seven-year-old stepson, Charles Edward Cotton.

Her sisters-in-law were not the only ones who had their suspicions. Thomas Riley, assistant coroner for West Auckland, was concerned at the unnaturally large number of deaths occurring in the Cotton household, and thought her demand for parish coffins excessive. Even before he was aware of her having 'lost' several husbands, he believed that even in those days of high child mortality, she had either been unbelievably unlucky or must have helped to send them on their way. He knew that she had recently become friendly with another man, and perhaps he wondered if she might soon need a coffin for him as well.

Early in July 1872 Riley visited her, ostensibly to ask if she could put her nursing skills to good use and help to look after someone in the area suffering from smallpox. This was surely subterfuge on his part, for in view of the recent history of those associated closely with her she must have been the last person to whom he would entrust the care of anyone. When he spoke to her, she asked if he would have room in the workhouse for her seven-year-old stepson Charles. It was hard, she said, for her to keep him when he was not her own son, and he was stopping her from taking in a respectable lodger. Well aware of village gossip, he said with a smile that she must be referring to the excise officer whom everyone said she wanted to marry. Evasively she replied that this might be the case, but her stepson was 'in the way'. Other neighbours had heard her say he was a tie and a burden on her, and she plainly resented having to maintain him. Although delicate-looking he was very active, but she told Riley she thought he seemed a sickly child and said resignedly that he would probably 'soon follow the others'. 'No, nothing of the kind,' Riley said reassuringly, 'he is a fine healthy boy.'

Mary Ann Cotton, a photograph taken shortly after her arrest in 1872

A few days later, as he was walking to work, she ran out of the house, clearly upset. He was astonished when she told him that little Charles was dead. As the lad had seemed in perfectly good health the last time he had seen him, Riley decided this was one premature death too many and informed Sergeant Tom Hutchinson of the local police force and the local doctor, Dr Kilburn. The latter was also surprised, as he and his assistant Dr Chambers had seen him five times that week for what they thought were symptoms of gastro-enteritis, but they did not think it would have been fatal. Dr Kilburn decided to withhold a death certificate, which prevented her from claiming the £4 10s insurance normally payable on his death, and asked for permission to carry out a post-mortem. The coroner arranged an inquest for the afternoon of Saturday 13 July.

Because of the pressure of other work, the doctors could not start the post-mortem until an hour before the inquest. After a brief and somewhat rushed examination on a table in Mary Ann Cotton's house, Dr Kilburn told the jury in the Rose and Crown next door that they found nothing to suggest poisoning. Death could have been due to natural causes, possibly gastro-enteritis. The jury returned a verdict of natural death, and the boy was buried in a pauper's grave. She indignantly accused Riley of blackening her good name by creating suspicion in others.

However, an uneasy Dr Kilburn shared Riley's concern, and had taken the precaution of preserving the contents of the boy's stomach in a bottle. On 17 July he undertook some tests, found distinct traces of arsenic, and took the results to the police. Charles's body was dug up and sent to Leeds School of Medicine, where Dr Thomas Scattergood, a lecturer in forensic medicine and toxicology, found more arsenic in the bowels, liver and lungs.

Meanwhile Riley undertook some investigation into Mary Ann Cotton's family history and found out about the other sudden deaths. On 18 July she was arrested, charged with Charles's murder, and held at Durham Gaol. The scandal was too much for Quick-Manning, and he walked away from the woman who was carrying his unborn child. On 21 August she appeared at Bishop Auckland Police Court, facing a charge of wilful murder 'by administering arsenic or causing it to be administered' to her stepson, and she was committed for trial at the next Durham Assizes.

Frederick Cotton's brother Charles, who lived in London, had already been in contact with Sergeant Tom Hutchinson of the West Auckland Police, to voice his suspicions about

*Mary Ann Cotton (*Illustrated Police News*)*

his sister-in-law. On 9 October he wrote Hutchinson a letter which was widely quoted in full in the national and regional press.

In consequence of the many reports which I have read, and which have (as it appears) been brought to light through your vigilance concerning Mary Ann Cotton, I am suspicious of her having had some acquaintance with my brother's family previous to the deaths of his first wife, two of his children, and also his sister, the latter having left her former service to keep house for my brother (F. Cotton) about or soon after the time that the above deaths occurred. At that time they resided at No. 5, Devon-row, Walbottle Colliery. I do not know any person who was living in that neighbourhood at the time above mentioned, or I would write with a view to obtain such information as might dispel or confirm my suspicions. My sister, Margaret Cotton (as I was informed by my brother Frederick), died very suddenly with a severe pain in her stomach, but the other three had a more lingering death.

I wrote to you on the 1st of September last, but did not make any remarks as to whether such letter was to be treated officially or merely private, but left it to your discretion what use to make of it; but I trust you will not be silent with regard to the contents of this.

On 14 October 1872 Superintendent Henderson, of the Durham County Police, received an order containing a warrant from the Home Secretary, authorising the exhumation of the bodies of Frederick Cotton, her late husband, who had died on 19 September 1871, two days after their first wedding anniversary; his ten-year-old son Frederick, who died on 9 March 1872; and their own son Robert, aged fourteen months, who died on 28 March. Their bodies, as well as those of Charles Cotton and Joseph Nattrass, had been interred in St Helen's churchyard. Those of Charles Edward Cotton and Joseph Nattrass had already been disinterred and examined by Dr Thomas Scattergood of Leeds, who found enough arsenic in them to kill them.

Although Mary Ann Cotton was pregnant again, she could not expect to escape from the long arm of the law. It had been decided that if poison was found in the viscera of her late husband and two children, another charge would be preferred against her in regard to the deaths of these three persons, and she would also be charged with the wilful murder of Joseph Nattrass. All the evidence would then be fully examined. As a result, it was probable that any inquiry instituted by the Durham county magistrates would be extended to another group of deaths near Sunderland with which it was alleged she was connected, as she had attended on them during their last sudden illnesses, and had a financial interest in the deaths of most of them.

The medical men representing the Durham county justice, acting on the authority of the Home Office for the exhumation of the bodies of the three Cottons suspected of having been poisoned at West Auckland, began searching for bodies in the churchyard of St Helen's on the morning of Tuesday 15 October, shortly after 4 a.m., and lasted for almost twelve hours. They only found two, those of the children, Frederick and her infant child Robert, and their search for that of her husband Frederick, interred in September 1871, was in vain. The sexton who pointed out the graves was elderly, no comprehensive register had been kept and the deaths had occurred during an epidemic of smallpox without any regard to future identification of the graves. The men therefore had nothing to depend upon but his memory, and as he directed them to burial places which once open proved to contain coffins which were not wanted, the search had to be given up. The two bodies were easily identified after the exhumation, taken to an outhouse, the viscera

Mary Ann Cotton's house, West Auckland
© Paul Head

were removed and put into jars, sealed up, and taken by police to Dr Scattergood.

On 20 October it was confirmed that Mary Ann Cotton had no connection with the death of her husband's first wife, or the children of Cotton's sister, at Walbottle, near Newcastle-on-Tyne. The sister had died in March 1869, and it was not until 7 July that the then Mary Ann Mowbray came to the village, met Frederick Cotton, became his housekeeper, and shortly afterwards his wife. The only accusation against her while she was a resident at Walbottle was with regard to the neighbours' pigs being poisoned, where she was the first to accuse them of having poisoned the animals, though they taunted her with having killed them herself. A second attempt was made on Thursday 17 October to find the body of her husband Frederick, interred in St Helen's churchyard, Auckland, but after the police and medical men had examined several graves without success they gave up.

The second investigation before the magistrates at Bishop Auckland was expected to be into the deaths of James Nattrass, in whose body arsenic had been found, and the children, Frederick and Robert Cotton. It was thought that the authorities would not extend their enquiries for the time being any further than to determine the deaths of the three Cottons, sons and father, and Nattrass. An investigation had already been completed into the death of Charles Cotton, as a result of which Mary Ann Cotton was in Durham Gaol awaiting trial. The evidence in these cases, it was thought, would be complete enough to make it unnecessary to pursue a complete judicial investigation of all eleven deaths in the neighbourhood of Sunderland for which she might be responsible.

Nevertheless it was established that between 1860 and 1871 Mary Ann Cotton had four husbands, namely William Mowbray, George Ward, James Robinson and Frederick Cotton. Three had died suddenly, two allegedly of fever, and twelve children of the families with which she had been connected as wife or mother also died suddenly, but according to the medical certificates, of fever. They were attended by medical men in good practice, yet none of them seemed to have had any suspicion of foul play or considered contacting the police. The only people who had felt something was wrong were Mr Robinson, his family and Mr Riley. Mr Gammage, who had attended Elizabeth Mowbray when she was ill, said she had died of gastric fever. In this he was supported by the surgeon Mr Shaw, who had attended the Robinsons.

The magistrates ordered Mary Ann Cotton to stand trial in December for the murder of Charles Edward Cotton. As she would have been about eight months pregnant at the time, and in view of the possibility of further charges to be brought against her, the trial was postponed. On 10 January 1873, while in custody, she gave birth to a daughter, who was named Margaret Edith Quick-Manning Cotton.

On 21 February she was committed to Durham Assizes, charged with having murdered her stepsons Charles and Frederick, her own child Robert, and Joseph Nattrass. An examination took place in the courthouse at Bishop Auckland. While in court she held her baby in her arms all the time, listening calmly and attentively to each witness, but did not ask any questions.

In opening the proceedings, Mr W. D. Trotter, clerk to the magistrates, stated that from analysis made after all the bodies concerned had been exhumed, it was established that they had all died from arsenic poisoning. Although the evidence was circumstantial, it could be proved that within a few days of the death of Nattrass the prisoner was found in possession of arsenic.

The first witness called was George Vickers, a pitman at West Auckland, who had known Nattrass and seen how ill he was about three days before his death. Thomas Hall, a colliery overman under whom Nattrass worked, said he saw the deceased on the Sunday before his death in the prisoner's house, where she was attending to him. He said that in the same room as Nattrass, in a coffin, the body of the child which had died on the previous Thursday was there. When he asked her why she did not bury the child, she said there was no hurry as Nattrass would probably not live for much longer.

Phoebe Robson, wife of a pitman at West Auckland, said that she had frequented the prisoner's house for some time, and knew that Nattrass had complained of being sick and having pain in his bowels. The prisoner, she said, was attending him very closely and would not let anybody else do so. When Mrs Robson suggested he would be better with more support and nourishment, the prisoner replied that he could not take anything. During the last few days of his illness he often had violent fits in which he clenched his hands, ground his teeth and drew up his legs. She (Robson) once heard the doctor say that he did not understand these attacks, and while he was having them Mrs Cotton held on to him tightly. The latter said that as he was not going to live very long, she could have him and the child buried together.

Several other neighbours gave evidence which confirmed this testimony. Dr Scattergood confirmed that the results of his analysis had convinced him arsenic poisoning was the cause of death. Elijah Atkinson, a shoemaker, said he had been sent for on the Thursday before Nattrass died, and asked him whether he intended Mrs Cotton to have all his effects. Nattrass affirmed this, 'as he had no friends who had ever looked at him'. Atkinson drew up a will to that effect, to which Nattrass added his mark. He had a watch hanging at the head of his bed, and £10 of sick money in the Oddfellows' Club, which would be payable at his death. Mrs Cotton was in the room while the will was being made. John Ayre, a miner, said it was one of his duties as an Oddfellows' steward to pay the sick and burial money for the Oddfellows' Lodge at Shildon, of which Nattrass was a member. £10 would be payable at his death, as well as nine days' sick money, an extra 15s. She claimed the money, and he paid her £5 15s. Robert McNaughton, a trustee of the Oddfellows' Lodge, said he paid to the prisoner the remaining £5 of Nattrass's burial money.

Dr T. C. Richardson, who attended Nattrass during the illness, said that after treatment for internal irritability and pain in the bowels he thought the patient was getting better, as did the patient himself. The symptoms, he was sure, were consistent with arsenical poisoning.

Thomas Detchon, a chemist's assistant at Newcastle, said that in January 1869 a woman calling herself Mary Ann Booth had come with another woman to the shop and bought 3d worth of soft soap and arsenic. That woman was the prisoner, and he pointed her out at an identity parade among a dozen women at Durham Gaol in November 1872. Jane Hedley, formerly a neighbour of the prisoner, said she had often helped Mrs Cotton with household work while Nattrass was ill and soon afterwards. On one occasion, about a week after he died, Mrs Cotton recommended a composition of arsenic and soap, with which to clean the beds. The witness went to the prisoner's house and found it there.

After this evidence for the prosecution, Mary Ann Cotton was formally charged, and when asked if she had anything to say she replied, 'nothing at present'. She was committed for trial at the next Durham Assizes, beginning on Saturday, 1 March.

Hearing of evidence as to the poisoning of the two children was then adjourned until the morning of 25 February, when proceedings opened with Mr Trotter reading out a letter from Charles Murray of Stockton, offering to take means to have her defended at Durham Assizes. It was handed to her, and she gave it to Mr Smith, whom she had engaged to defend her. She asked him to reply to it and accept the offer with thanks.

The case of Frederick Cotton, who had died on 10 March 1872, his treatment for enteric fever, his symptoms of illness and purging, were examined. Dr Kilburn and Dr Scattergood both confirmed the presence of arsenic in the viscera. On behalf of the Prudential Assurance Company, James Young said that the deceased was insured for £5 15s, and Robert Robson, Charles Edward Cotton and her husband Frederick Cotton had all been insured in the same office. Again she said she had nothing more to say, and she was committed for trial at the next assizes.

She was then charged with the murder of little Robert Cotton on 29 March. Dr Kilburn said he had first seen the infant early in the morning, apparently in good health, on his mother's knee. Although he admitted that there had been a rapid change in him on the last day of his life, he said this was not unusual, as 'children sometimes die in teething before a medical man can be brought'. Even so, he was astonished to hear that the boy was dead, for the last time he saw him he looked well enough. Mary Ann Cotton had refused to call in neighbours when his symptoms appeared, excusing herself by saying that she knew the child was dying and she wanted him to be left alone so he could die quietly. At the end of the examination the prisoner was committed on a charge of wilful murder in each case. During the hearing she complained that the person to whom she had entrusted her defence was not fulfilling his duty, and the bench assured her she would be provided with an able counsel.

The three-day trial at which she was charged with the murder of her stepson Charles Edward Cotton opened at Durham Assizes on 5 March under Mr Justice Archibald, with Mr Charles Russell, QC, Mr Greenhow, Mr Bruce and Mr Trotter as counsel for the prosecution, and Mr Campbell Forster for the defence. After she had pleaded 'not guilty', Russell outlined the facts as he saw them and the family history, emphasising that she found her stepson a burden to maintain, and that his life was insured.

At one point, he said that with the sanction of the judge he should offer 'extensive evidence', but anticipated that there might be an objection from the defence and would do no more than indicate the evidence. 'I have told you that three children and the husband...' Campbell Foster rose to his feet, and the judge said firmly to Russell, 'You have done enough; leave the details.' The problem about the admissibility of evidence regarding other deaths in the household, which would have been seen as prejudicial to the outcome of the case, would overshadow the entire trial.

After Russell had finished, a succession of witnesses gave evidence. Among them were Isabella Smith, who had been a nurse with the prisoner at Sutherland Infirmary, the latter's neighbour Mary Ann Dodds, Thomas Riley, and the prisoner's cleaner Mary Ann Tate. Everything they had to say proved thoroughly damning, particularly Mrs Tate's observations about the prisoner not giving the boy enough to eat and thrashing him hard with a leather strap.

On the second day of the trial, much of the evidence was taken up with medical evidence. Mr Scattergood said he had found traces of arsenic, a total quantity of 2.60 grains, in the contents and substance of the boy's stomach, bowels, liver and kidneys. He believed that repeated doses of arsenic had been administered, some shortly before death, as traces were found in the stomach. Two to three grains would cause death in an adult, half that amount for a child. Dr Richardson, who had treated Nattrass in his last illness, said he had never expected his patient to die. He thought the lodger had had kidney disease, but not severe enough to have caused his death within two or three days. A few other witnesses were called before Russell closed the case for the prosecution.

On the third day of the trial, Russell insisted in his summing up that the evidence of three other cases of death by arsenic in the prisoner's house, within three months of the death of the child which was the subject of inquiry, proved it was a case of direct and deliberate administration of poison. The prisoner had treated the child badly and complained that he was a burden on her, as well as an impediment to any chances of her marrying again. She had tried to have him admitted to the workhouse, but was told this could not be done unless she also went in to the workhouse herself. Not only did she have a financial interest in his death, as he was insured for £4 10s, but she alone looked after him, and thus had every chance to poison him. At the infirmary she had also been able to acquire a working knowledge of the nature of drugs and poisons, and how to administer them. Kilburn and Scattergood had given evidence that the child had died from the effects of arsenic, as had two other children and Mr Nattrass. Although there was no absolute proof that she had administered it herself, there was little doubt that she had done so, and if so she was therefore guilty of murder. It would be 'dangerous and alarming' if a case of the strongest circumstantial nature was to be considered doubtful merely because there was no direct evidence of the prisoner's possession of poison.

For the defence, Mr Campbell Foster then asked the judge to strike out the whole of the evidence relating to the other three deaths, as possession of poison had not been proved. He said there was little point in asking the jury to dispel all prejudice from their minds, and to form their opinion on the cause of facts proved pertinent to the issue. Every newspaper in the country had carried reports of the case, and evidence had been given of three previous deaths in the prisoner's house from arsenic — for the sole purpose of prejudicing their minds; though not proved, it was strongly inferred that the poison had been administered by the prisoner.

Had she been convicted of these crimes after due enquiry before a jury, the law would not have allowed such evidence to be given on the basis that it would sway the minds of the jury in the verdict they had to give in the case. Any substantiation of the prisoner's cruelty amounted to no more than chastisement of the child with a leather belt and rested mainly on the evidence of three or four 'gossiping women'. Cross-examination revealed that each of them had a belt, a whip, or a 'taws', which they used on their own children for punishment. Moreover, when the deceased was examined after death there was not a single mark or bruise upon him. Any insurance benefits to be derived by his death would be more than lost by the funeral expenses (though he omitted to add that she had regularly claimed poor relief, and it was arguable as to whether she was morally as well as legally entitled to collect it). Once the child had been taken ill she had sent immediately for Dr Kilburn, and he and his assistant had attended him daily until his death. Their evidence, and that of the charwoman who waited upon her and the child, all proved that she showed the boy great kindness. If the prisoner's experience in hospitals had taught her anything about poisons, she would have been aware that the skill of the medical men would soon detect them, and yet the doctors who attended her family were sent for as soon as the child became ill.

It had been established that the children had died from the effects of arsenic, and that the prisoner had obtained some six weeks before, mixed with soft soap, to be rubbed into the joints of a bug-infested iron bedstead. Mrs Dodds had used nearly all of it, a quantity containing about 300 grains of arsenic, over the steel lathes of the bedstead and in the joints. It had been proved by Dr Scattergood that after four or five weeks the mixture of the soft soap spread over the bedstead would dry and it would become hard, the rubbing of steel lathes over each other whenever a person got in or out of bed would rub down the dry soap and arsenic into dust, and it would fall on the floor. The room was decorated with a wallpaper containing arsenic, which had been known to cause chronic arsenical poisoning.

Dr Scattergood estimated that the four walls of a small room papered thus might produce twelve grains of arsenic dust rubbed off, and any inhalation of the dust and minute floating atoms could cause illness. Every time the child ran around the room, played with toys or jumped into bed, a cloud of these poisonous atoms would be dislodged and inhaled by the 'delicate, susceptible boy'. Much of the matter inhaled would adhere to the tongue, mouth and throat, and be swallowed. After five days and nights, it was hardly surprising that as much as 26 grains of arsenic had been found in the child's stomach after death.

Further evidence proved that the child had been locked in the house alone, yet the soap and arsenic had not been put away in a jug. Such a dwelling probably did not boast many jugs. If they were not rinsed out thoroughly, deposits would remain in the vessel, as it would take several thorough rinsings to remove all traces of arsenic completely. The child might have thus accidentally drunk water or milk from the jug, and inadvertently been poisoned that way. It was also proved that when he was ill a prescription had been made up for him by Dr Kilburn and Mr Chalmers's assistant, consisting of bismuth and prussic acid. These poisons were on the same shelf as and close to the arsenic bottle, so it was possible that some unfortunate mistake might have been made with the bottle and that this arsenic might have been administered as medicine.

Despite the strong prejudice introduced into the case, he ended with an appeal to the jury to give the prisoner 'fair play'. It was possible, he said, to conclude that the child had inadvertently taken the arsenic, and it did not follow that the prisoner had deliberately poisoned him without any apparent motive. She had treated him kindly and sent for the doctors when he became unwell. It was hard to reconcile this with the picture of a scheming woman watching day by day the agonies for which she was responsible, and of which the doctors could not discover the cause, and had then put on a hypocritical display of grief at the loss of the boy whom she had killed. 'Our common nature revolted at such a picture as an impossibility. It was far more consistent with reasonable probability that accident or mistake had led to the child having taken arsenic than that a woman capable of such conduct could exist.' If the jury was in any doubt, they should find the prisoner 'not guilty'. His address lasted almost two hours, and when he had finished, Mr Hardy, one of the reporters, applauded. Mr Justice Archibald called him to order for such an 'indecent manifestation' and threatened to send him to prison for contempt of court until he apologised.

After retiring for almost an hour, the jury returned with a verdict of 'guilty'. When the judge passed sentence of death she seemed stunned by the verdict, fainted in the dock and had to be helped out of court. The trial had occupied three days. As three clear Sundays had to pass between sentence and death, her execution was scheduled for 24 March. Had she been acquitted of the charge, the prosecution were ready to put her on trial for the murder of Joseph Nattrass.

Next day, the *Newcastle Journal* referred to her as 'a monster in human shape', with no less than twenty-two deaths mentioned in the police report. 'Murder grew with her...We feel instinctively that the earth ought to be rid of her.'

On 12 March she wrote to Mr Robinson, and like several of her other letters it soon appeared in the press, at first locally and then in *The Times*. Reproaching him for having turned her out of the house, she begged him to try and help save her:

...And I think if you have Won sarke of kindness in you Will Try to get my Life Spared you know your sealfe there has been a most dredfull to hear tell of the Lyies that has been told A Bout me ie must tell you Ar th Cause of All my trouble fore if you had not Left th house And so As i could have got into my house When i came the dor I Was to Wandr the streets With my baby in my Armes no home for me no plase to lay my head you Know if you call your mind Backe i should not solde my things in susicke street to come to you....Won thing i hope you Will try to get my Life spared for ie Am not guiltty of the crime ie have to dyie fore consider things And do What you Can fore me so ie must conclude at this time i hope to hear from By return of post...

Like Quick-Manning, Robinson was no longer prepared to be involved with her, and he did not reply.

There was the matter of providing for little Margaret Edith, who was now two months old. The mother had kept her baby in a cradle in the cell, and the prison authorities were presumably satisfied that unlike most of the rest of her children she would be relatively safe from the prisoner's basest motives. Nevertheless, after the death sentence was pronounced, there were rumours that she might deliberately try and make the child ill in order to delay her execution until the child had recovered. Her cell was regularly searched, and one day it was found that a small piece of soap was missing. Prisoners often swallowed soap, as it had a purging effect and could cause a low fever. When questioned about it she said she did not know what had happened to it (though she could surely have said she had used it up for its usual purpose), but when she herself was searched it was found up her sleeve.

She had hoped that the father might take his child, but Mr Quick-Manning had refused to have anything more to do with his former mistress and their daughter. However, once the word had got around, there were many families who came forward, eager to adopt the hapless infant. It was said that there were over 150 applications, among them a Justice of the Peace and his wife from Bishop Auckland. Mary Ann Cotton was allowed to choose, and she decided her daughter should go to Sarah and William Edwards, a childless couple in their late twenties from Bishop Auckland who had been married for seven years. They assured her they would bring her up as a good God-fearing child. The couple and Mary Ann's last lodger, William Lowrey, came to take Margaret Edith on 19 March. Apart from the infant whom she abandoned shortly after James Robinson had ordered her out of his house and his life in 1869, this was the only one of her twelve children to survive her.

Petitions were launched to try and obtain a reprieve, on the grounds that there was very little direct evidence against her and that she could not afford to call upon expert legal advice to challenge the evidence of Dr Scattergood, but to no avail. On the evening of 19 March, Lowrey wrote to the *Northern Echo*, describing his visit with Mr and Mrs Edwards to the gaol earlier that day. He mentioned he had received a letter from Mrs Cotton about a week before, asking him if he would try and get up a petition to save her, but he told her he thought she had no chance. The only advice he could offer was that she should 'come to the cross of Christ, for he says, "Let your sins be as red as scarlet, I will make them as white as snow, He that cometh unto me I will in no way cast out."'

On 22 March, she had her last visitor from outside, her stepfather George Stott, and he later gave an account of their meeting to the *Northern Echo*. When he was shown into her cell, she was gazing at the fire. She jumped up, hugged him tenderly and said she knew that he would come to see her. He told her, wrongly as it turned out, that the petitions raised on her behalf had not been forwarded to the Home Office. The bad spelling and grammar in her letters published in the papers had surprised him, and she must have lost the benefits of the excellent education she had had as a child. She excused herself on the grounds that she had too many other things to think of, and in view of her unhappy position it was not surprising.

Maintaining her innocence, she conceded she might have been instrumental in causing the death of Charles Edward, after buying arrowroot from a grocer in West Auckland, and he had made up the quantity with something else of a different colour from another drawer. This, she said, had poisoned the boy. If the shopkeeper was partly responsible, he answered, why did she not say so at the time? When she replied that she was 'confused', he told her that she had had one of the best counsellors in England and she should have mentioned the matter to him. She said she had entrusted her defence to an attorney, and he advised her to say nothing.

When the subject of her mother came up, he would not divulge any more, apart from the fact that 'her wicked habits tended to shorten her mother's days'. His stepdaughter admitted she was guilty of bigamy, but when 'that bad man Robinson drove her to the door' she had no alternative. After promising her that he would try and see Robinson on her behalf, he got up to leave. He could hear her crying for some considerable distance after leaving the cell. Having brought her up from childhood, he said he knew that she would not confess to anybody but him, and that if she was guilty, she would die without making a confession — as indeed she did.

Mary Ann Cotton was executed by William Calcraft and his assistant Thomas Evens early on the morning of 24 March 1873. After she had been led to the scaffold and 'launched into eternity', according to some of the papers after a few convulsions the body was motionless. Others reported with lurid detail that it was three minutes before the more or less violent movements of the condemned woman weakened to mere twitching, and that her frame was 'terribly slow to yield the last sign of life'. After a formal inquest, two members of the West Hartlepool Phrenological Society took a cast of her head, by permission of the justices, in the interests of scientific knowledge, and facsimiles were to be sent to Durham Gaol and to a scientific society in Edinburgh. She was buried beside Hugh Slane and John Hays, the last two convicted murderers buried there.

William Calcraft, chief hangman between 1829 and 1874, who executed Mary Ann Cotton as well as the Spennymoor killers

As Calcraft and Evens were leaving Durham, people gathered at the station to stare at them. When they entered their carriage, Calcraft had to draw the curtains across the window to stop crowds from looking in.

It was said that Mary Ann Cotton's past history and the suspicion of other murders being laid at her door could have brought undue influence to bear on the jury. Her moving from place to place under different names had undoubtedly diverted attention from the deaths in her wake. William Mowbray and two of their children may have died of natural causes, as did possibly four more of the children. Her motive was in each case related to money, or the lack of it; children and adults were killed so she could attract a better, probably more wealthy, husband, be free of an idle one or one who could not work, or collect insurance money. It was sometimes acknowledged that life insurance could have a detrimental effect on the welfare of children, and — as her case sadly demonstrated — act as a positive incentive to unscrupulous parents to despatch them. Poisoning was often difficult to detect and could often be done easily without leaving trace, in times of high mortality. Only when success went to her head, in particular when she was rash enough to predict the demise of the apparently healthy Charles Cotton to a third party, who then became suspicious of the unusually high number of deaths connected with her, did this astonishing 'success' run out.

CHAPTER 5

'I'LL FINISH HER'

Darlington, 1873

Charles Dawson was an ironworker by trade, though like many other employees in his position he found that poaching and taking in lodgers were far more lucrative occupations. He had left his wife, who lived in Stockton, and was living with another woman, Martha Addison, aged about twenty-four. A native of Barnard Castle, she had been living with him for about two years. She earned a living by making ginger beer, which she sold to a local shop, generally earning between 30s and £2 per week.

At about 5 p.m. on Saturday 13 September 1873, Dawson, Addison, Thomas Mullen and two other lodgers went into Darlington, shutting up the house at Cleveland Street, Albert Hill. Dawson and Addison became separated when she called in to see a cousin, who had recently got married, and then visited a shop. Dawson and Mullen tried to find her but could not, then went back to Albert Hill. As they were crossing the railway near the house where they lived, they met her coming from the town. Without saying a word Dawson knocked her down and said that when he had got her indoors he would kill her.

They continued towards the house, and when they entered Dawson said he would give her a few minutes to pray for her soul before he killed her. He then hit her hard on the head with a bottle, and she fell to the floor. Before she could get up he threw another bottle at her and kicked her in the ribs. Mullen, who was present all the time, said that she continued to scream when Dawson kicked her several times, pressing her neck down on the floor with one of his boots and kicking her in the ribs with the other. He then jumped on her chest and her neck, walked over to the fireplace, picked up a coal rake and hit her several times.

As he also had a revolver, Mullen was afraid to intervene. Meanwhile Patrick Dempsey, another lodger, walked in and told Dawson to leave her alone. 'The cow, I'll finish her,' was his retort as he picked up a large earthenware pan full of dirty water, threw the contents over her and then hit her in the face with it, knocking several of her teeth out. When he ordered Mullen to fetch him some clean water, Mullen went outside to the tap, filled a pail, laid it on the doorstep, and then ran to the police station. He returned with Superintendent Rogers and Constable Stokoe, but they found the house locked and the blinds pulled down, with no sign of Dawson or Dempsey, and they had to force their way in. Martha Addison was lying dead on the floor with a pillow beneath her head, and the blood which had covered her face had been washed off. The room, spattered with blood, was covered with the remains of the bottles and the earthenware pan with which he had attacked her.

Several groups of police had been called to keep a watch on roads around the town, and to search a number of what were known to be his regular haunts. Sometime after 2 a.m. the next day Sergeant Cuthbert, searching at Albert Hill, saw a dog which he knew belonged to Dawson. The dog led him to a building and scratched at the door. Dawson was inside, sitting on a chair with his head down. Though it may have been his dog, it evidently knew the difference between right and wrong. He was still armed with a revolver with six chambers, but did not offer any resistance. Cuthbert told him he was charged with murdering his wife. 'I know that, sergeant,' Dawson answered. 'I have done it; oh dear, oh dear, I can't help it now; it's a bad job.' He was taken to the police station and locked up. Two guns and two pistols, one loaded, were also found in the house where the murder was committed.

On Tuesday 16 September Dawson was taken before the magistrates and gave a short statement prior to being remanded in custody. When he was read the witnesses' statements, he said they were full of lies. He was then taken in a cab to the Allan Arms, Albert Hill, where the inquest was to be held. Crowds had gathered in the street, and as the vehicle drew within sight there was much booing and hissing. According to the papers, he was 'a small man, but well knit, and has a determined-looking aspect' and had been 'at times greatly affected since his incarceration and has eaten little or nothing, and presents a dejected appearance'.

The first witness to be called at the inquest was his father-in-law William Addison, a labourer, whose heartrending task it was to identify the deceased. He was followed by Rachel Newton, a widow who lived nearby, and said that Margaret Addison and Dawson had called at her house around 7 p.m. on the day of the murder. The latter was noticeably the worse for drink. They were quarrelling in her house about an hour later, and Dawson struck Addison with the palm of his hand on the side of her head. However, she did not retaliate and it did not look as though he had hurt her. He left soon afterwards and returned to Mrs Newton's house about 10 p.m. Addison had gone, and he said, 'If I light on her I'll make her that she'll not run away again'.

She was followed by Mullen, who confirmed that he, Dempsey and 'Benny' Harper used to lodge at Dawson's house, and that Dawson and Addison lived together as husband and wife. He described their night out together that Saturday, how they had gone into Northgate and how Dawson had made several purchases. Dempsey and Harper left them at a butcher's shop, and they met a bricklayer, a friend of Dawson. The four of them went into Brown's beerhouse, where Dawson bought two quarts of ale, none of which Addison drank. She and Dawson then left them to carry on to a wedding party, and he appeared still sober at the time. After Dempsey joined Mullen and the bricklayer at the beerhouse they had another drink.

A little later Mullen and Harper met Dawson against the railway bridge, coming towards the town on his own. He said he was going to look for 'his wife', evidently meaning Addison, and asked Mullen to accompany him. They called in at various places on their way, including the house where they had attended the wedding party. As they walked along the railway line and the crossing beside the South Durham Blast Furnaces they met Addison, coming from the direction of the town.

To Mullen's horror, Dawson struck her with his fist behind the ear and knocked her down, then lifted her up by the arm. She had done nothing to provoke him, and though she cried out in pain she did not say a word. They walked in silence back to the house, and as they reached the front door Dawson told her to unlock it. As she was about to put the key in the lock he took it from her, unlocked it himself and they went indoors. He put the key in his pocket, took off his coat and waistcoat, threw them on the bed, and lit a candle. Once it was burning, Mullen noticed that Dawson had a revolver in his hand, and told him that if he raised the alarm or spoke to anybody 'of what I saw him do, he would put the contents of the revolver into me'. When one of the jury asked Mullen why he stood by without trying to intervene or protect her, Mullen said he was afraid to, as he knew Dawson was capable of carrying out his threat.

Next in the witness box was Dempsey, who corroborated Mullen's version of the evening's events. He admitted that when he came back to the house on his own, between 10 and 11 p.m., he was 'the worse of liquor'. Perhaps the alcohol had given him the courage that the more sober Mullen lacked, for he told Dawson that he had killed her, and he himself would go for the police. 'You had better go for the doctor,' Dawson snapped. Dempsey took her hand but could not feel a pulse, and he assumed that she was dead. Nevertheless he went for Dr William Easby, who could do little more than confirm the fact.

After this the jury heard medical evidence from Dr Easby and his assistant George Middlemiss, who had helped at the post-mortem and confirmed that the cause of death was an effusion of blood on the brain, which might be produced by a blow from a hard substance, or being felled violently to the ground.

The jury took little time to return a verdict of wilful murder. As it was pronounced the prisoner uttered a loud groan.

For the second time in less than a year, the *Newcastle Courant* weighed forth in expressing revulsion at the brutality shown in this murder of a defenceless citizen:

That peculiar and terrible form of murder that is so frequent in the county of Durham, the kicking to death with heavily weighted quarter-boots, has had a rather aggravated illustration this week in Darlington, where the fellow that did that villainy actually stood with one foot on his paramour's neck, while he kicked the life out of her with the other foot, after which he smashed in the features of his victim with the coal-rake, a workman lodger actually looking on until all was finished, afraid to interfere! Already this year the lives of two of the kicking murderers of Durham, which the law had adjudged to be forfeit for their crimes, have been spared from the gallows; and now, in September, we have a crime that passes beyond the others in fiendish atrocity; for the Spennymoor murderers did but kick their victims to death, the Willington murderer kicked and jumped upon his victim; in this case, the paramour is held under one heel, while the other foot kicks out the life. 'When he got tired of this,' says the poltroon who saw and spoke not, 'he jumped with both feet on her stomach. He jumped up and down on her stomach about half-a-dozen times without going on to the floor.' Should the law in this case declare a murderer's life to be forfeit, I feel assured that justice will have its due.

On 17 September Dawson agreed to his household goods being sold in order to defray the expenses incurred as a result of his crime. The necessary steps for carrying out his instructions were taken by Sergeant Cuthbert. During the afternoon, the borough bellman walked through the streets of Darlington, announcing clearly that Richard Trees would be selling the household effects of Mr Dawson 'and his unfortunate paramour' and the dog at 3 p.m. that day by auction at Cleveland Street. The sale lasted about three hours. A large quantity of articles and utensils for the manufacture of ginger and herb beer found ready buyers. A 'stout bludgeon' and a sieve for making ginger beer went for 1d each, and the dog fetched 6s 6d. Beds and bedding were also snapped up, 'evidently intended for houses whose residents were not of the too sensitive class'. It was observed that there was no special demand for relics, and the 'morbid element' was evidently absent.

Mullen was present and 'was made the object of some inconsiderate chaff'. He explained that there were extenuating circumstances. Only aged twenty, he had previously been in a foot regiment of the army but was sent to hospital after becoming ill. A chronic incurable chest condition and palpitation of the heart had been diagnosed, and he was discharged on health grounds. Moreover he was genuinely afraid of being shot and killed by Dawson, and he had no access to any weapon in order to defend himself or even attack him if necessary. He was well aware that Dawson always carried a loaded revolver with him whenever he went poaching.

Dawson appeared at Durham Assizes on 11 December. After Mr Justice Honyman had heard the evidence originally produced at the inquest, he asked Dawson whether he had anything to say. 'I have not had a fair trial,' was the reply; 'there are many things that might have been mentioned which were not mentioned.' Donning the black cap to pass the death sentence, the judge said it would be a waste of time to advise him to prepare for a better place, 'as mercy both in this world and in the world to come was lost to him'.

On 20 December, while under sentence of death in Durham Gaol, he wrote to his parents, a letter reproduced in the press as written:

I got your letter this morning. I am in good spirits, and you need not knock yourselves about, and try to keep up your hearts for I will keep up mine, for I have not anything to be afrade to die for, for I can say with a honest hart that I did not know what was done

William Marwood, hangman from 1872 to 1883, and thus responsible for all executions in Durham between 1874 and 1878

to the woman that night, for if I wished to be parted from her was it not in my power to turn her to the door any time I wanted, if she had gone home with me first when she seed that I was in such a state, no doubt this would never of happened her conduct has not been right it is plane to see. But I can die happy for her I had non wish to cause her death, for I thought to much of her for that I would have been sorry to parted with her I never could have been in my mind to do anything like that to the woman I thought so much about only a few minits befor God knows I wished her well we went down the town as happy as could be, plenty of things for the coming week, and how this come about I cannot tell. It cannot be helped now, so you must not believe any tales that is got up about her and me, for they will try to make all sorts of lies up. It grieves me that I cannot be buried beside her. I do not know anything that need be afraid to die, for I can say before my maker with a honest harte that I had non wish to kill her for she was a good woman to me and therefore I can die happy for her.

Dawson was one of three convicted murderers hanged in a triple execution by William Marwood at Durham on 5 January 1874.

CHAPTER 6

THE BOTTLE OF PORTER

Marley Hill, 1873

On 7 July 1873 Edward Gough, a twenty-two-year-old pitman, walked into a public house in Sunnyside village, near Marley Hill, and ordered a small bottle of porter. James Partridge, a fellow pitman, was already there drinking with a group of rather noisy friends. 'What is the use of ordering a small bottle of porter,' he asked Gough; 'won't you order something we can all share?' Ignoring him, Gough drank his porter in silence and left.

A little later he returned with a companion and challenged Partridge to a fight. After some argument, both men went outside and were followed by several others. Partridge took his coat off in readiness for a scrap. Gough was standing between two men, who were well aware how dangerous he could be when provoked, and were trying to prevent the men from coming to blows. Suddenly he ran at Partridge, drew a jackknife from his coat and stabbed him on the inner side of the thigh. Partridge shouted out in agony and ran to the opposite side of the road, pursued by Gough. He fell to the ground and was dead within quarter of an hour. A post-mortem revealed that the blow had divided the femoral artery.

The police were alerted, Gough was arrested and taken into custody. A short, thick-set man, he was brought up on 8 July at Gateshead County Court, charged with the killing. When asked how he wished to plead, he made no answer. Superintendent Wood briefly stated the facts of the case, and applied for a remand in order that the prisoner might be charged before Chester-le-Street magistrates. Constable Lancaster, who had apprehended Gough, said that when charged after the killing, the prisoner said, 'They have put me into it.' The remand was accordingly granted, and at the inquest on Wednesday 9 July, the jury returned a verdict of wilful murder against Gough.

At the Durham Assizes on 13 December 1873 the case was heard before Mr Justice Honyman. Acting for the prosecution were John Edge and Mr A. Liddell, and for the defence Mr Skidmore.

The defence tried to argue that when Gough struck Partridge with the knife it was not premeditated, and amounted to no more than manslaughter, 'owing to the prisoner having acted under passion and provocation', claiming that Partridge had asked for trouble by

*William Thompson, Charles Dawson and Edward Gough being led to the gallows at Durham Gaol, 5 January 1874 (*Illustrated Police News*)*

mocking him. In summing up, the judge deprecated and denounced the prevalent use of the knife and other deadly weapons, particularly in Durham.

The jury were out for three quarters of an hour and returned a verdict of 'guilty', but with a recommendation to mercy on the grounds that the blow might have been inflicted in a moment of excitement. Gough looked totally unmoved as the judge sentenced him to death, informing him that the jury's recommendation would be forwarded to the proper quarter, but without holding out any hope of commutation.

Gough was executed with Charles Dawson and William Thompson, by William Marwood on 5 January 1874.

CHAPTER 7

'A BAD JOB'

Hetton-le-Hole, 1873

George Smith, formerly of Creitch, Derbyshire, moved to Durham around 1859. He came to Hetton-le-Hole, settled at 11 Barrington Terrace and married Miss White, who had a small daughter, Barbara Jane, from an earlier relationship. Barbara unwittingly proved a source of regular irritation between her mother and stepfather. In time they had seven children of their own, but Mr Smith, a heavy drinker, was often unpredictable in his behaviour towards the family. On at least one occasion his wife and children had to seek shelter or protection from their neighbours.

In April 1873, after one of his rages, Mrs Smith asked Mrs Bainbridge, who lived at No. 11, to come to her aid. The latter's husband, Michael, a pitman like George Smith, was very drunk at the time and followed his wife into the Smiths' house, while Smith called his wife several rude names. On a previous occasion, Smith had called Bainbridge his wife's 'bully', promising that he would 'put that fellow right, and blow his brains out'. A few months earlier he had been at the centre of a disturbance and was consequently bound over to keep the peace.

On Monday 15 September 1873 Smith came home from work later than usual and drunk, at about 7 p.m., sat down and began to cry. He then ordered his wife and stepdaughter, now aged fifteen, out of the house, saying he was not going to keep both of them. After an argument, they left and went to a neighbour's, taking the rest of the children. Smith followed them into his yard, saw Bainbridge at his own door, a short distance off, called him 'a knock-kneed bastard' and urged him to come out and fight.

Bainbridge refused the invitation, saying he had more sense than to go near him. His wife came, slapped Smith in the face and told him to stop taunting her husband about his wife or she would 'split his head'. Smith said he did not like to strike a woman, but if she did not go away, he would hit her. She then called to her husband to come and thrash Smith, but he still refused to come out. Smith then turned to the door of the next house, and called upon its occupant, John Reay, to come out and fight. Reay and Joseph Simpson, his brother-in-law, ran out, and a struggle then took place in the street. Smith, Reay and Simpson all ended up on the ground at one stage, and while they were down Bainbridge kicked Smith, then Ann Reay poured water on him.

His wife and stepdaughter got him away from the struggle and took him back into his own house. He ordered them out a second time and locked the door behind them. When Barbara looked through the kitchen window, she watched her father stand on a chair, take down a gun hanging on the wall, and load it. Tapping on the window, she begged him not to take it out of the house, but when she saw he would not listen to her, she warned everyone in desperation that he was arming himself.

Most of them prudently ran away, but Bainbridge and his two companions continued to stand a few yards off, on the far side of the street, directly opposite Smith's pantry window. Bainbridge defiantly called out to her, 'He dare not do anything with the gun; he's had it down before.' Some time then elapsed, variously given by different witnesses at from five to fifteen minutes, and then Smith's voice was heard from the pantry window calling out to Bainbridge, reproaching him again with bullying his wife.

Bainbridge called back to him to 'take down his gun' and then picked up a brick and threw it through the pantry window. Almost at once the muzzle of a gun protruded through the window, went off, and Bainbridge fell mortally wounded. The bullet had gone through his heart and bowels, and he died a few minutes later before medical aid could be summoned.

Somebody called the police, and Constable John Thompson arrived at Smith's house shortly after 7.30 p.m. to find a large crowd standing outside. The front and back doors were locked, and he shouted to Smith to open up. At first the latter refused to allow anybody inside. Thompson said who he was, to be greeted with a curt 'The first bugger that comes in, I will shoot him'.

'Well, don't make a bad job worse,' answered Thompson.

'What I have done, I did in self-defence. Three of them were kicking me.'

After further consideration commonsense prevailed and Smith agreed to open the door if the crowds promised to dispersed. Thompson asked them to leave, was allowed in and found him with the discharged gun still in his hand. He admitted it was 'a bad job', but he said he thought the gun was unloaded. Later he made the excuse that his gun must have gone off accidentally. After handing Thompson the weapon he was charged with murder, still pleading self-defence.

An inquest was held on 17 September at the Shepherd's Arms, Hetton, by the coroner, Mr Crofton Maynard. The first witness to appear was Silvester Thomas Wilkie, a brother of Mrs Bainbridge, who gave formal identification of the body of the deceased and confirmed his age as thirty-six. He had heard Smith threaten Bainbridge on several previous occasions. Next came Barbara White, who said that when her stepfather returned home on the day of the killing, he told her he did not intend to keep her any longer and she was to take her 'hook'. She went out and returned a little later. Her mother asked him if he would have any tea, but he declined the offer. After describing in some detail what happened next, she said that whenever he had the gun he was always more or less drunk. In April, her mother had had to intervene in order to prevent him from carrying out a threat to hang himself.

She was followed by Ann Reay, who had come out of her house after hearing a disturbance outside. She knew the family and told how three months earlier she had heard Smith threaten to shoot Bainbridge and his wife, saying that he knew he would be hanged.

The surgeon James Adams described how he had been called to see if anything could be done for Bainbridge but was too late as the latter was lying dead on his bed by the time he reached the house. During the post-mortem, he found the shot had penetrated Bainbridge's abdomen and chest. The three shots which had entered the heart would in themselves have been enough to cause death almost at once. There were also shot corns in the left lung, some of which he produced in court in a glass bottle, and the stomach and liver were also affected.

John Taylor, a mason, recalled that on Monday Smith was returning from work. He sat down beside him, found he was drunk, and talked about his family, how he had no control over them and how only three months earlier his wife had had him bound over to keep the peace. During their conversation Mason had mentioned the recent Darlington case in which Charles Dawson had been arrested on a charge of murder, and wondered what the end result would be. Smith muttered darkly that there would surely be a murder in Hetton that night.

Sergeant Thompson then spoke about his involvement with the events. He produced Bainbridge's shirts, riddled with shot and stained with blood, and a shot bag which had been laid open on the drawers in the front room, containing mixed shot resembling that which had been extracted from the deceased.

In summing up, Maynard said it was for the jury to consider as to the truthfulness of witnesses regarding the time that had elapsed between the time the brick was thrown through the window and when the shot was fired. Evidence given suggested that there had been an interval of ten to fifteen minutes, and if this was the case, the prisoner had had sufficient time to control his temper. In view of the element of premeditation, nobody was surprised when the jury retired briefly and returned a verdict of 'guilty of wilful murder'.

The case came to trial at Durham Assizes on 12 December 1873 before Mr Justice Honyman, with Mr Greenhow and John Edge conducting the prosecution, and Mr C. J. Fawcett and Mr Milvain for the defence. Upon being given the evidence, the counsel for the defence contended that, owing to the shape and position of the pantry window, which was half formed of a sort of sliding trellised panel, it was not proved that the gun did not go off accidentally while Mr Smith was trying to push aside the panel with the muzzle. It was possible that he had merely intended to frighten the men outside by presenting the gun, and that at most he had fired the gun under the influence of passion aroused by the unequal struggle in the street, 'which had not had sufficient time to subside'. Bainbridge had also behaved provocatively by throwing the brick, and if his aim had been better, it might have been him instead of Smith in the dock for murder.

After deliberating for over an hour, the jury returned a verdict of 'guilty of manslaughter'. Smith was sentenced to penal servitude for fifteen years.

CHAPTER 8

'WAIT UNTIL WE GET HOME'

Annfield Plain, 1873

William Thompson, a twenty-six-year-old pitman, and his twenty-year-old wife Jane lived at Felling, while he worked at Heworth Colliery. It was her second marriage. Her first husband, Henry Aitchison, had beaten her and eventually walked out, leaving her with a small child, which may have been born during an earlier liaison. Soon afterwards she met William Thompson, who proposed marriage to her. She was reluctant at first, and her family viewed him with deep misgivings, partly because they thought he was an unpleasant character and partly as she was still legally the wife of her first husband. However, when she learnt that the latter had taken a second Mrs Aitchison, she changed her mind and they were married at Gateshead Register Office in February 1872.

It was soon apparent to their neighbours that the Thompsons' marriage was unhappy, and the sound of noisy quarrels could often be heard coming from their house. He proved no better than her first husband, beating and starving her. When she found out she was expecting another child, she returned to her father Edward Johnson's house at Pontop Cottages, Annfield Plain, for a respite from his ill treatment until after the birth. He had cold-shouldered her when she married for the second time, but now he relented and readily forgave her. William Thompson followed her there, urged her to come home and promised he would mend his ways in future. There is, however, no record of when, or indeed whether, another child was born.

On Saturday 4 October all three left the house to spend the day in Newcastle, mainly visiting Jane's sister. She immediately noticed an improvement in Thompson's behaviour to his wife and remarked on it to them, at which he told her that he had given his word to treat her better in future than he had done in the past. They had a meal in a public house, and after they had eaten Jane noticed her cousin among a group of men nearby. She went over to speak to them, and Thompson took exception to her walking off without asking him first. During the journey home, the two women who shared a carriage with them were alarmed at the threats he was making as to what he would do to his wife when they were home again.

They arrived back at Annfield Plain about 7.15 p.m. and Mrs Thompson immediately began preparing supper, and a little later her father went to the inn, about five minutes' walk from their front door, for some beer. As Mr Johnson walked down the road, he was reassured to see that the couple were, in his own words, 'on terms more loveable than he had ever seen them in his life', convinced that any differences between them were now in the past.

He had only just arrived at the inn and given his order when one of the neighbours, Ann Scullen, ran in after him and told him that his daughter was lying dead on the floor of another neighbour's house. He had been walking past the Thompson's home when he heard a loud shriek, and on looking round he saw Thompson, dressed only in his yellow cord trousers and shirt, with no cap on, running away. Meanwhile Mrs Thompson staggered into the house of Ann Parker next door and collapsed on the floor. Mrs Parker found a large gash on her throat, but there was no sign of a pulse.

Thompson had tried to make himself scarce but was soon traced hiding in his brother Alexander's house in the neighbouring village of Tipton. As he was led away by Sergeant John Brown he wept bitterly, remarking over and over again that it was 'a bad job' and he could not tell whatever had made him commit the crime. A sudden fit of temper, it was apparent, had made him pick up a knife and attack his wife. She immediately tried to run away but he was too quick for her. As she reached the footpath outside the house he overtook her, seized her by the shoulder, and cut her throat, severing the muscles and arteries to within quarter of an inch of the right ear. The head was very close to being severed, and when an attempt was made to raise the body it fell backwards and rested between the shoulders, remaining attached to the body by the vertebrae alone.

Remarkably, though she was in effect killed a few yards from Mrs Parker's home, she had apparently 'by the mere force of muscular action induced by excessive panic' staggered some considerable distance before collapsing on the ground. Moreover, although the carotid and other arteries were severed by the knife and a large quantity of blood was found on the victim's clothes and around where she was stabbed, there was none on Thompson's clothes.

Thompson was brought before the magistrates at Shotley Bridge Police Court on 6 October. When charged, he said she had taken a razor and tried to murder him, and then killed herself in a fit of remorse. Shortly after being examined he was taken to Annfield Plain, where an inquest was held by the coroner Mr Favell.

The first witness to be called was Ann Watson. She had been to Newcastle on business that Saturday afternoon, and on the return journey she sat in Mr Bone's horse-drawn carriage, between Mr and Mrs Thompson. On the way, he accused his wife of having spoken to a man in Newcastle: 'You bitch, you are all right with him; did your cousin tell you when he was going to take you away.' He then hit her in the face, and she retaliated in kind, at which he threatened her, 'Wait until we get home, and it will be either you or me for it.' She snapped back, 'Wait; it will be either you or me for it. You are not going to murder me. You always commence to abuse me when my father goes out.'

Annfield Plain, West Street

This story was corroborated by Sarah Graham, another Annfield Plain resident, who had also been in the carriage with them that afternoon. As they reached Pelton Bank, she said, Thompson got out of the brake, and walked up the bank. She turned to Jane, saying, 'Is that your husband?' She nodded, 'Yes, the villain; he is jealous of me because I spoke to my cousin in Newcastle.' He got into the brake again, and on reaching Oxhill he asked his wife for some money. When she refused to give him any, he said, 'I will be all right with you when we get home.' As they left the brake on reaching Annfield Plain, he hit her in the face with his fist. She returned the blow and began to cry, telling him, 'You always use me so when my father is out at night.'

Edward Johnson then came to the witness box to say that the three of them had had supper at about 8 p.m., and he then took a quart jug to Mrs Dodds' public house. As he left, his daughter and son-in-law were sitting at the table, apparently on good terms. About ten minutes later Ann Scullen came to bring him the tragic news.

Other neighbours spoke of having heard the victim scream and her husband running away. Sergeant Brown, stationed at Annfield Plain, testified to having searched for Thompson, finding him in his brother's house and taking him into custody at Consett for the night. Constable Joshua Reay, stationed at Oxhill, spoke of having examined Edward Johnson's house at about 9.30 and finding everything in good order there, with no marks of blood on the floor. He had helped to bring the prisoner from Consett earlier that day. A colleague of his, Constable Stamper, was told by the prisoner that at Newcastle on Saturday he and his wife had gone to a public house for a meal. Some men from Pelton Fell were there and she went to join them, leaving him sitting at the table on his own 'like a child'. On their return home they had some words, he put his arms on the table and laid his head on them. As he looked up, he saw his wife with a razor in her hand. He got up, she ran to the door, he followed her and struck her.

The last witness was John Hunter, a surgeon from Stubb House who had carried out a post-mortem on Jane that morning. There were no external indications or bruises, but he

Annfield Plain, Wesleyan Church

found a deep wound inflicted on the throat, extending from the left part of the lower jaw to about an inch behind the right ear, the wound being high up on the throat. The main arteries of the throat and the larynx had been completely divided, and she would have bled to death within two or three minutes.

Thompson was asked if he had anything he wanted to tell the court, but declared he could not 'say anything against myself'. After the jury had retired briefly, they returned a verdict of wilful murder, and he was taken back to the lock-up at Consett police station.

On 23 October he was placed in the dock at Lanchester Police Court before Chairman Mr A. Kearney and Mr A. Town, charged with murder. In his statement to the court, he said that on their visit to Newcastle his wife Jane had gone out with a man and left him sitting on his own for half an hour. After waiting, he went out to see if there was any sign of her. From a distance he could see her, but there was no man nearby. After they got home that evening and her father went out for the beer, he spoke to her angrily about 'not being with a man' again in future, and she retorted that it was no business of his whom she was with. When she threatened him with a razor, he ran after her and struck her on the head. She ran about two yards and he saw blood streaming down, and he then went to his brother's house.

He was then committed to take his trial at the next session of Durham Assizes. Shortly after he was removed to the cell, Superintendent Oliver returned into the courtroom carrying a piece of tow rope, about four feet long, which he had just confiscated from the prisoner. Before Thompson's removal, a policeman in court had noticed a man behind him give him something, and being suspicious, he warned Oliver. Thompson was searched and the rope was found on him.

It was commented on by the press that he had changed considerably in appearance since he was last in court. He was sleeping badly, seemed to be suffering mentally, and was convinced that the witnesses were prejudiced against him. As he was taken back to his cell, he angrily accused them of having 'laid their heads together' in order to give evidence that would prove unfavourable to him. He was taken from Lanchester by the 4.40 train to Durham Gaol that afternoon.

The case was heard before Mr Justice Honyman, on 15 December 1873, with Messrs John Edge and Sowerby for the prosecution and Mr Sidmore for the defence. Most of the witnesses had been present at the previous hearing. One who was there for the first time was Ann Thompson, wife of the prisoner's brother Alexander. She said that Jane Thompson had been very afraid of her husband, and she herself thought the man was 'a lunatic' because he had such a wild look.

For the defence, Mr Skidmore said that Jane Thompson must have been afraid of the consequences of her misconduct, and through the prisoner suspecting her he submitted that she committed the rash act that led to her death. If they could not arrive at that conclusion, he asked them to say that the prisoner was guilty of manslaughter, and that the wound was inflicted by the prisoner in consequence of provocation from the deceased.

In summing up, the judge said that the outcome of the case depended on whether the wound was inflicted by the prisoner at the bar or the deceased woman herself. If there was an element of provocation, it would have to be very serious if the charge was to be one of manslaughter.

The jury retired for forty-five minutes before returning a verdict of 'guilty'. When the judge asked Thompson if he had anything to say, he answered, 'Well, sir, if I were to die this present moment I am not guilty, I am innocent, sir — '

'Do you wish to say anything else?' asked the judge.

The prisoner did not, and the death sentence was accordingly passed. Before being removed from the dock, Thompson said, 'The Lord will protect me.' Several women in court sobbed bitterly.

A few days later Thompson, full of repentance, made a full confession of his crime to the Revd J. C. Lowe, the prison chaplain. His brother and sister came to visit him at the gaol on New Year's Day, and on 5 January 1874 he, Charles Dawson and Edward Gough all went to the gallows.

CHAPTER 9

'DO YOU WANT TO TAKE THIS MAN'S PART?'

Howden, 1874

On 2 November 1874 Edward Tipping, a thirty-three-year-old labourer, and his friends, Smith, Mooney, Adams, Stephenson and Richardson, visited the Australia Inn at Howden. After drinking there for about an hour, they left and went towards Bitchburn Square. On their way, they stopped for another drink at Mr Adamson's inn. While they were there an altercation took place between Mrs Smith, Tipping's mother-in-law and some of the others. Adams then left and visited two more hostelries in quick succession. After leaving the second he called at Mooney's house at Bitchburn.

As he came out of the front door, he was about to go to Tipping's house next door, when Tipping walked up to him and knocked him down; without giving him a chance to retaliate he kicked him hard as he lay on the ground. Adams hit his head and was unconscious for a while. Eventually he came round, picked himself up and walked away. Where he went was not quite clear, but on his way he met Patrick Duffy and several other friends, and they all went to Mrs Smith's house, where Tipping had gone after his attack on Adams.

Before going into his mother-in-law's house, Tipping called at Goodwin's inn, and then went to Mrs Smith's house. He had not been there long before Adams came up and asked why he had attacked him. Tipping said he was prepared to hit him again, or he would fight any person there. He then turned to Duffy and asked, 'Do you want to take this man's part?' Duffy said he wanted nothing to do with them, but he was not prepared to stand by and see Adams being abused like this. Tipping said once again that he would fight Duffy or any of those with him, or indeed the whole lot of them. Going back into the house, he came out again without his coat, and said he would fight the deceased for a sovereign, offering to give him two sovereigns if he could thrash him. If Duffy was prepared to fight the prisoner, would he put up his hand? Duffy refused to accept the challenge, and he and his companions turned to go away from Mrs Smith's house, keen to leave before the situation turned ugly. Mrs Smith then came to the door and cried,

'Tipping is ready for you, come back and have a fair fight, and I will hold the candle.' Duffy and the others returned to the house. Meanwhile Tipping had gone indoors, only to come out again almost at once, carrying a coal rake. Without another word he put his hand before Duffy's face to shield his view, and struck him hard with the rake. Duffy fell to the ground immediately, and before a doctor could be called, he was dead.

Tipping was arrested, taken into custody and charged at Durham Spring Assizes on 4 March 1875 before Justice Baron Pollock with the wilful murder of Patrick Duffy. Mr Skidmore and Mr Granger prosecuted, while Mr Edge and Mr Sowerby conducted the defence. In opening the case for the jury, Skidmore said both the prisoner and deceased were coal drawers, living at Bitchburn Square or Thistleflat. Tipping, he continued, had armed himself with a weapon and launched an unprovoked, fatal attack on Duffy. Edge contended that it had been a tragic accident with no malice aforethought.

Though the prosecution had argued forcefully that the killing of Patrick Duffy had been premeditated the jury were inclined to agree with the defence; Tipping was found guilty of manslaughter, and he was sentenced to five years' penal servitude.

CHAPTER 10

'MASTER OF MY OWN HOUSE'

Dipton, 1874

The Daleys of Dipton were one of several Irish families who crossed the North Sea in the mid-nineteenth century for a better life in England. Simon, the eldest of the brothers, came to settle near Durham about 1857. Hugh followed four years later, with brothers John and Peter and two sisters arriving shortly afterwards. Hugh lived with Simon at Bushblades for a while and became very friendly with his wife's sister Mary. They lived together, had a son and a year after that they were married at Leadgate. Later in their marriage whenever Hugh became drunk he would accuse her of infidelity and of having deceived him over the paternity of the child.

In November 1874 Hugh and Mary Daley's family consisted of two boys, of whom the eldest was aged eleven, and three girls, the youngest being aged seven months. He drank heavily, and when he was in his cups not even his own brothers would go near him. He and Philip Burdy, a fellow miner who soon became a friend, often went out drinking together. Mrs Daley always dreaded it when they returned from a session, their breath smelling of alcohol, as he would taunt her about her eldest son, whom Burdy rather mischievously spoke of to Daley as 'someone else's bairn'. Daley usually ended these exchanges by striking his wife and son, unless they had the good sense to leave the house first until he had sobered up. As Daley used to spend most of his wages on drink, the family often went hungry. When her husband became really quarrelsome, Mrs Daley tried to persuade Burdy to leave the house before he returned. She and her children were receiving relief from the parochial authorities but still found it hard to make ends meet. Simon Daley was unable to assist her financially, as his business was going through a difficult time.

On 7 November 1874 Hugh returned from a day's work at the pit to his house at Dipton, stopping at an inn on his way, and was very drunk by the time he got home. His wife gave him a meal, and then their neighbour, Ann Smith, helped her put him to bed to sleep it off. When Philip Burdy entered the house, Daley woke up, jumped out of bed and picked up an iron poker. Burdy ran outside, Daley followed him and beat him violently about the head and left him lying on the ground insensible, then went back into the house. Ten minutes later he came out again, took the poker in both hands and in a fit of frenzy battered the bleeding head of the unconscious Burdy until Constable Forster, alerted by neighbours, arrived to arrest him. Burdy was carried into Daley's house and Dr Hunter was sent for, but the wounded man died about half an hour later.

On 9 November Daley was brought before Mr Annandale Town at Shotley Bridge, and charged with Burdy's murder. When Daley had attacked him, two or three other men were present, but they were afraid to interfere because he had a reputation for being violent. Constable Forster said that he ran about a mile after being told what was happening. From some distance away he could hear the sound of blows being rained down on the unfortunate victim's head. Coming a few yards closer, he heard Daley swearing at his victim and ordering him to get up. When he saw Forster, he said he had just killed one man and would do the same to him as well. Although he aimed a blow with the poker at Forster's head, it struck the ground, he lost his footing and the policeman pounced on him and handcuffed him.

On 10 November an inquest was held by the coroner, John Graham, at the Prince of Wales Inn, Flint Hill, Dipton. Mrs Daley was present and gave the impression of being quite unconcerned. The first witness, John Power, another miner, at East Pontop Colliery, said he was in Smith's public house at Dipton on the day of the killing and found Daley there. He was sitting in the tap room and already seemed the worse for drink. Although any sensible friend might have supposed that such a man with a reputation for violence and bad temper had already had enough, he still sat down for another drink with Daley. Between 2.30 and 3.00 p.m. they left the inn and went on together to High Bushblades, by which time Daley was even more in his cups. They arrived at his house about 4.30 p.m., and on arrival he saw a man whom he did not recognise lying drunk on the floor of Daley's house. The man turned out to be Burdy.

The only other person he noticed in the room was Daley's wife, and she had a young child in her arms. A little later Mrs Smith entered and asked him to go for a policeman. When the coroner broke in to ask Power where he was at this time Power admitted, a little shamefacedly, that he was in Daley's house, as Simon Daley had asked Power to protect her. 'A nice protection you would be,' retorted the coroner. 'You are a thorough coward.' Power then said that he showed his face as soon as Forster arrived. Burdy was lying three or four yards from Daley's door, and bleeding from the head and face.

Ann Smith said that at 5.30 p.m. she went to Daley's house, four doors away from where she lived. She had heard there was trouble, went to see what the matter was, and found the unconscious Burdy on the ground outside the front door. A wound on his head and scratches about the face, covered with blood, were clearly visible. She fetched some water from Mary Daley and washed his wounds, then (rather bravely, one would think) helped Daley inside his house, gave his wife a hand to take off his coat and vest as he was incapable, and they put him to bed.

Ten minutes later Burdy staggered weakly into the porch at the entrance to the house, and asked for his cap. Daley leapt out of bed, went to the fireside and took a poker,

Durham Gaol, c.1930 © Sunderland Echo

remarking as he did so that he would make Burdy leave the house. He struck Burdy on the head again and knocked him down. Mrs Smith begged him to leave the poor man alone but he took no notice of her. When she could bear it no more she went to Simon Daley's house for help. Simon went to fetch a policeman. During that time the prisoner was going from door to door, using bad language and asking everybody where his wife had gone. She presumably had the good sense to keep out of his way for a while. Burdy lingered on without regaining consciousness and died of his injuries at about 8 p.m.

Constable Henry Forster said that at 6.15 p.m. Simon Daley informed him that a man had been murdered. He secured the prisoner and then told Simon Daley, William Smiler and another man to carry Burdy's body into Hugh Daley's house. To the prisoner he said, 'Hugh, you have done a bad job; you have killed the man, and he is lying dead before you.' 'I have killed the bugger,' snapped Daley, 'and I'll kill him again. I will allow no man to go into my house; I am the master of my own house.'

John Gillard Hunter, surgeon and physician at Stobb House, near Dipton, said that he saw the body of Burdy lying on the floor in front of the fireplace. His head, face and hair were covered in blood. He was comatose and still breathing feebly but beyond all medical assistance. A post-mortem concluded that death was caused by concussion and compression of the brain. Although Burdy had known the family well for some years, Mrs Daley, described by the press as 'a poor, thin, innocent-looking creature', was anxious to let it be known that she did not think jealousy had anything to do with her husband's reason for the murder.

Daley appeared at Durham Assizes on 11 December before Mr Justice Cleasby. The evidence against him was overwhelming and the jury took little time to agree on a verdict of murder. While he was in Durham Gaol awaiting execution, Mary and the children never came to visit him, ostensibly as they could not afford to make the journey. His brothers John and Peter, who were also miners at Haswell Moor, both came to say goodbye to him. He told them he wanted to see his wife and family, so it seems a little surprising that they did not come together. He was hanged on 28 December.

Bad blood evidently ran in the family. Two months later, on 27 February 1875, at Castle Eden Police Court, Peter was brought up in custody of Constable Walker, charged with assaulting him in the course of his duty at Haswell Moor on 6 February. In court Walker said that the defendant was partly naked, 'running his wife about' and threatening to murder her. Walker intercepted him, and Daley felled him with a single blow. 'I will murder you,' he vowed. 'I have had one brother hung for murder, and I'll be hanged before the year's out.' He was fined 40s and costs for assault, plus 2s 6d and costs for damaging the policeman's helmet. The defendant's wife refused to prefer a charge of assault against him. Nevertheless he did not succeed in following his brother to the gallows, either in 1875 or in any subsequent year.

CHAPTER 11

'WHAT'S MINE'S MINE, AND WHAT'S THINE'S THINE'

Gainford, 1875

James Watson, a Gainford labourer, and his wife had brought up her niece, Elizabeth, after she was orphaned at an early age. Elizabeth lived with them until she married, becoming Mrs Pearson, and settled down with her husband nearby. When Mrs Watson became ill, she returned to her uncle's house with her young child so she could help with the nursing. After her aunt died in the spring of 1874, her husband came to join her and they shut up their previous home.

On 15 March 1875 Mr Watson passed away at the age of seventy-four. Nobody had any reason to suspect anything other than natural causes until an inquest was held at the Lord Nelson Inn on 16 April by Thomas Dean, the deputy coroner. It then became apparent that his death had been hastened.

The first witness called was Ann Hall, whose husband Robert was a groom of Gainford. At 5 p.m. on Monday 15 March she had been invited into the house by George Smith, a fisherman who was lodging with Watson. When she walked in, she saw Watson upstairs in bed, looking very ill, while Elizabeth was holding his wrists, saying she thought he was going to have a trembling fit. Watson begged Mrs Hall not to leave him. 'No, James, I won't,' she said, 'but we must try some remedies.' She asked Elizabeth if there was any brandy in the house, only to be told that he had had the last of it that morning. She thought he needed some brandy and a hot-water bottle to warm his feet. He looked as though he was cringing, with his head thrown back, and he was holding himself together. His teeth were not set, and she did not notice any trembling. When he gave a loud groan, he said he 'could not tremble it out'. That was the last time she ever heard him speak.

She went downstairs to fetch some hot water so she could apply bottles to his feet, but before she could return Elizabeth Pearson told her to hurry back. Going upstairs at once, she found him quite still, his teeth set, his eyes fixed as in death, and his hands folded over his chest. A slight heaving of the chest confirmed that he was still alive, and she told

Elizabeth Pearson to call George Smith. When he arrived she left the room. She said that in all the eight years since they had known each other as neighbours, she could never recall him having had a fit before.

Evidence from the physician and surgeon Francis Hamilton Homfray was read. He said he thought the deceased was suffering from a spasmodic fit, though there was nothing in the general appearance of complaint for which he was treating him that would cause such symptoms. On 19 March he placed part of the stomach and liver in a glass jar in the presence of Superintendent Thompson, sealed it in three places with his own crest, and handed it to Thompson for safe keeping.

Thomas Scattergood was given the jar on 23 March and said it contained a hum in the stomach, opened by a cut three or four inches long, the contents of which had escaped into the jar. There was also about one foot in length of large intestine, attached to the stomach by a piece of omentum, and an 8½ oz portion of liver. The intestine was healthy, and contained solid faeces, and the stomach likewise appeared normal, apart from one small patch of bright redness of the mucus membrane. However when he analysed the liver, intestines, and stomach, he found traces of strychnine in each, the substance of the stomach containing more than ½0th of a grain. The liver contained a much smaller quantity, while the intestine only showed a trace, as did the contents of the stomach, while the solid part of the contents of the stomach consisted chiefly of meat in small pieces, undergoing digestion. He found granules of starch, quantity ⅟₅₅ of a grain, in an unbroken state and particles of blue colouring matter, analysed them and found they were Prussian blue. There was no other poison to be found in any of the articles he examined, no calomel in the stomach, neither any mercury in the liver.

On 14 April he received by post from Thompson a letter containing two 3*d* packets of Battle's Vermin Killer, in yellow envelopes. When he checked them, he found they contained flour, strychnine and Prussian blue. While he did not find enough strychnine in the parts which he examined to constitute a fatal dose, he was sure that there was more strychnine in the body than the amount he had found. A smaller dose than the usual amount which would prove fatal to a vigorous middle-aged person would certainly kill an old and feeble man. He also confirmed that Mrs Hall's description of the symptoms suffered by the old man were consistent with strychnine poisoning.

The next witness, John Corner, a grocer at Gainford, said that the prisoner's mother-in-law Jane Pearson called regularly at his shop. On two separate occasions, on 2 March and about a month previously, he sold her two 3*d* packets of Vermin Killer, which she told him were for her daughter-in-law Lizzie. When she bought the second lot, he asked her jokingly if she intended to poison herself. She told him the first packet had been bought to kill mice and it had helped her to dispose of about a dozen, so she needed another for the same purpose. Elizabeth had asked her not to say anything to Elizabeth's husband, as he did not like the idea of poison around the house.

FATAL FACILITY; OR, POISONS FOR THE ASKING.

CHILD.—"PLEASE, MISTER, WILL YOU BE SO GOOD AS TO FILL THIS BOTTLE AGAIN WITH LODNUM, AND LET MOTHER
HAVE ANOTHER POUND AND A HALF OF ARSENIC FOR THE RATS (!)"
DULY QUALIFIED CHEMIST.—"CERTAINLY, MA'AM. IS THERE ANY OTHER ARTICLE?"

** The ease with which poisons could be purchased from druggists, afforded a menace to human life. Some fatal cases had recently
come to light.

'A Fatal Facility; or, Poisons for the Asking', by John Leech,
published in Punch, 8 September 1849, a comment on the ease
with which poisons could be purchased

When all the evidence had been heard, the coroner summed up and cleared the room.
Mr Raine, the foreman of the jury, said they needed further evidence before arriving at a
verdict. Proceedings were resumed when Mary Brown, the wife of Christopher Brown, a
Gainford mason, said he was in Watson's house on the morning of his death. Watson told
him he felt a great deal better and was going to get up. Elizabeth Pearson gave him a little
wine, which he drank without any apparent ill effects.

After the room was cleared again reporters were admitted, and the foreman said the
jury had decided the deceased died from strychnine, administered by his niece. When
the coroner told her she would be committed for trial on a charge of wilful murder, she
betrayed no emotion as she told him she would be calling witnesses on her behalf. She
insisted that she was not guilty.

On 8 July 1875 she appeared at Durham Assizes before Mr Justice Archibald, who thus found himself presiding over the second trial of a woman charged with murdering by poison within less than three years. Mr Skidmore and Mr Milwain led the case for the prosecution, Mr Ridley for the defence.

The first witness to be called was the prisoner's mother-in-law, Jane Pearson. She said the deceased had always been very fond of 'Lizzie', telling everyone that he was 'never better visited on in his life' than he was with the prisoner. She did not think they were on bad terms about other members of the family, or indeed anything at all as far as she was aware. For some time the deceased had suffered from chronic inflammation of the lungs, and was thus more or less an invalid. However, a doctor was not called in until 6 March, nine days before he died. The prisoner told him that her uncle suffered from trembling fits.

Next to give evidence was Robert Watson, son of the deceased. On 13 March he had come from his home in Barnard Castle to see his father. When Robert and the prisoner were discussing the old man's state of health, Robert said he wanted his father to give up his house and go into lodgings, or else stay with him. When asked for his view, James Watson said he wanted to spend the rest of his days in Gainford. Robert then said that if it really was his intention to settle there, he would make him an allowance of 4s or 5s a week, but he would have to sell his furniture. When he spoke about removing his father to Barnard Castle, she told him she had been warned by the doctors that his father would never come downstairs alive again.

After Robert went downstairs, Elizabeth followed later to tell him that his father had changed his mind and agreed after all to going to live with him at Barnard Castle.

Two days later, James Watson was dead. Robert went to his father's house, and on his way he met the prisoner's husband's sister carrying some clothes horses. On arriving at the house, he found all the doors were locked. By the time he had managed to make his way in, at about 9 p.m., the place was in darkness. Nevertheless he struck a light and could see his worst suspicions confirmed. The house had been stripped of nearly all the furniture, linen, clothes and bedding. All that was left was one single bed, with his father's body lying on the bedstead bars. A pillow was beneath his head, but all the bedding had gone.

Next day he saw Elizabeth Pearson at her own house and asked for his father's money so he could bury him, as he understood his father had had some savings in the house. 'You said you would bury your father,' she told him coldly, 'you can bury him now.' When he asked her how she meant him to do so, she laughed. Feeling he was not going to get any cooperation from her, he left the house angrily. About one and a half hours later she saw him again. He then contacted the landlord of his father's house, and both of them visited the premises together. The landlord confirmed that there was still 10s for rent outstanding. They then went as one to the prisoner's house and the landlord asked her to pay the sum. When she laughed and said it was impossible for her to do so, he threatened to take her to court.

After leaving the house, Robert went to the station and found the prisoner's husband, and they visited the Pearsons' house together. In the prisoner's presence, he asked Robert Watson if he would be content with what James Watson had already signed on to Elizabeth Pearson, meaning the furniture. Robert Watson said he would, and Mr Pearson said he would certainly let him have them. At this Elizabeth broke in, saying she did not agree and she would rather make firewood of them first. Then she said, 'What's mine's mine, and what's thine's thine, and what I have I'll stick to.' Robert could see some of his father's furniture in her house. Although since then he had been able to acquire the furniture which was rightfully his, he still had none of the linen or the bedding. Later Mr Pearson sent for him and he got the furniture, but the husband still could not find what she had done with the linen or bedding. It was then pointed out that James Watson's second wife had predeceased him by about a year, and it was through his second wife that he had acquired much of the furniture.

Other witnesses reiterating evidence already given included Mary Brown, who lived next door but one to James Watson, Ann Hall, Dr Humfrey, and James Scattergood.

After all the evidence had been heard, Mr Milvain summed up for the prosecution by arguing that the deceased had died of strychnine poisoning and that it had been administered by the prisoner. There had been rumours that George Smith the lodger might have been the guilty party, but none of the witnesses called ever saw him waiting on the deceased. Though he had left rather suddenly and could not be traced, that in itself was hardly good reason to lay this dastardly crime at his door. He had no possible motive, let alone any opportunity of administering the poison. The prisoner's motive was evident; there was definitely jealousy between her and the deceased's son about the ownership of the furniture, and before Robert Watson had a chance to lay his claim, Elizabeth Pearson had coveted the lot for herself.

On behalf of the prisoner, Mr Ridley argued that there was no clear proof that James Watson had died from strychnine poisoning. Everything in the case, he said, was left to conjecture, from the cause of death having been the administration of strychnine, to the circumstances and motives under which it was administered. He contended that the medical evidence had failed to establish conclusively that the deceased's death was caused by strychnine at all, and that if it did, there was no proof that the strychnine had been administered in the shape of Battle's powder and by the prisoner. The poison might have been contained by mistake in powder sent by the doctor and taken by the deceased, but no remains of that powder had been found in either of the houses. Battle's powder could have been given to him in error, or by somebody else, possibly the lodger, George Smith. His hasty disappearance after Watson's death, he argued, made it far more likely that he was the murderer.

Finally, he contended that there was no motive for the prisoner to commit such a crime. She had been better off in her uncle's lifetime than after his death, as until then she and her husband had lived rent-free. She had every reason to expect that her uncle's furniture would pass to her after his death, as it would then become her rightful property.

The jury retired for thirty minutes and returned with a verdict of 'guilty'. When the judge asked if she had anything to say as to why sentence of death should not be passed on her, she said, 'Yes, sir,' but made no further comment.

The judge then told her:

It is a crime of very deep dye — the poisoning of your uncle, who seems always to have treated you with affection, and to have reposed in you the greatest confidence. There is evidence from which the only conclusion one can draw is that you have made the most elaborate preparations for this crime, and carried it out to its accomplishment. Crimes of this character are undertaken and endeavoured to be carried out in secret; but it so happens in the order of Providence that, though the crime is secret, it is the one, of all others, that may be said to write its own history in the traces it leaves, which science now enables us to decipher, and to read without doubt or uncertainty.

As he sentenced the twenty-eight-year-old convicted murderess to death, she showed no sign of emotion. She went to the gallows on 2 August in a triple execution conducted by William Marwood, alongside Michael Gillingham and William McHugh.

CHAPTER 12

THE DEATH OF MRS TULLY

Throston, 1875

On 15 March 1875 forty-two-year-old John Tully, a labourer, attacked his wife Bridget at their home at Throston with a poker. She was admitted to the local infirmary, where she died on 24 March.

After the doctor examined her, he gave his opinion that her death had not been caused by violence on the part of her husband. At the time of the attack she had already been ill with inflammation of the lungs from pleurisy. Although Mr Tully had inflicted injuries on her, he said, these had not hastened her death. Nevertheless he was charged with the wilful murder of his wife.

The case was heard at Durham Summer Assizes on 10 July before Mr Commissioner Russell, with Mr Skidmore prosecuting and Mr Blackwell defending. Initially the prisoner had been committed on a charge of wilful murder, but the bill was thrown out and a charge of causing grievous bodily harm was taken instead.

For the prosecution, Jane Fewster, a neighbour, said that on 15 March she had heard loud screams coming from the Tullys' house. When she went round to see what was wrong, she found Mr Tully with a poker in his hand, about to strike his wife. She was lying on the floor, while he was holding her by her hair, in which his hand was 'entwined', and he also kicked her in the bowels.

On the next day, her attention was alerted once more when she heard the daughter screaming. When she went round to the house she found Mrs Tully back on the floor, bleeding from the mouth. She got the poor woman up, and once Mrs Tully had recovered she complained that her husband had attacked her. Mrs Fewster returned home, but later that same day she heard a noisy argument between husband and wife. When she went round and asked Mr Tully what the matter was he said that his wife was threatening to drown herself. Subsequently Mrs Tully was discovered with both eyes discoloured and a bruise across the nose. In answer to Mr Blackwell, she said she saw the prisoner strike his wife in the mouth, as well as holding her by the hair.

Their fifteen-year-old daughter, Ellen Tully, said she saw her father take up the poker to strike her mother on 15 March, but she ran out of the house and did not see him strike her. On the next day he struck her mother across the nose and on the side of the head, causing her to stagger and hit her head badly on the wall. Her mother went out into the yard, but her father brought her back indoors, by which time she was bleeding from the nose and the head.

Another neighbour, Elizabeth McLinney, corroborated the other witnesses, adding that there had been some differences about financial matters. He threatened to kill her, and twice she saw him kick his wife while he was wearing a pair of heavy boots.

Dr Morrison of Hartlepool had been called to attend to Mrs Tully on 17 March, when she complained of a pain in the right side and leg. He found a bruise on the right part of the shin, but not much the matter with the side. Her head was bandaged with a cloth, and she was sporting two black eyes. He was present at the post-mortem, and over the right ear he found an effusion of blood as well as discoloured skin around the eyes. Nevertheless he did not attribute her death to the injuries. His evidence was corroborated by his colleague Dr Gourley.

Although not convicted of murder or even manslaughter, John Tully was found guilty of assault, and given nine months' imprisonment with hard labour.

CHAPTER 13

DEATH IN A DARLINGTON STREET

Darlington, 1875

On the evening of 28 March 1875, forty-two-year-old John Kilcran, a labourer and local secretary of the Hibernian Society, was attacked at Darlington. Six or seven Irishmen, who were assumed to be Fenians, were seen lurking at the corner of one of the main thoroughfares on Sunday night, evidently looking or lying in wait for somebody with whom they had an old score to settle. When one man walked past they looked into his face, before satisfying themselves that it was not him whom they were looking for. Then Kilcran appeared, and in the dim light he evidently looked like the one. Michael Gillingham, the leader of the group, struck him to the ground with a heavy instrument, leaving him with a fractured skull. The other men kicked him as he lay prostrate on the ground and ran away.

Kilcran was carried home, with a fractured skull. He was still just conscious, and when the police interviewed him he managed to give a description of his assailants. Gillingham and two others, James Durkin and James Flinn, were charged with assault and taken into custody. Meanwhile Kilcran's condition gradually deteriorated and he died of his injuries on 8 April.

An inquest the next day returned a verdict of wilful murder against his assailants, and they went on trial at Durham Assizes on 8 July under Baron Eddlestone. Gillingham was found guilty of murder and sentenced to death, while Durkin and Flinn were charged with aiding and abetting him. Both were found guilty of manslaughter and sentenced to fifteen years' penal servitude.

After being sentenced Gillingham left a letter to his brother Michael:

I now rite these Few lines to you in return to your Kind and affectionate letter I am very happy to hear that yours are all in good health dear brother, you Can only get to see me on friday, for the last time, if you can come, and if not, you will rite me your last ferwell, but, if you by any means, I should like you to come and pournance the last words of ferewell with me at Durham, as that fatal hour is drawing nie whitch is to take my Innasend life away dear brother, I am not relying upon a resprive, but if it is the goodness

Darlington, c. 1850

and liberality of the gentlemen of darlington to gain it for me, and if the beleve that I am not the man, I wid receive it with a smile, but if the think that I am still the man, and wishes to sue for mercy for me, I wid reather died than bare the name of a murderer, for my god still stande by me, and will cheere up my wounded heart, and will give me curage for to die my dear brother, I hope you will looke with kindness towards my poor mother, which I lave broken hearted behind me as I cannot expect you to do anything for my poor wife and children, I hope here friends will recive here Still with Kindness, as this fond heart that now lies in chains can never more return to assist here I now send you my kind and affectionate love, and may god asist my poor wife and mother, and sister, and too children so I will bid you good night for the present, and will write again.

On 10 July it was reported that a petition was being organised by friends of Gillingham, to be sent to the Home Office, asking for the Secretary of State to issue a reprieve. This was on the grounds that he had always proclaimed his innocence, and that he was supported by Durkin, who swore that he was not present when the murder was committed.

It was to no avail, and he was hanged by Marwood on 2 August.

CHAPTER 14

'I WILL BE CLEARED BEFORE GOD AND MAN'

Barnard Castle, 1875

On the evening of Saturday 10 April 1875, a group of friends gathered at an upstairs room in Fryer's Yard, off Bridgegate, Barnard Castle, for a drinking session. It was a small place, about fifteen feet by fourteen feet, in a house rented by William Gallagher, a thirty-five-year-old labourer. He was a widower with four small children, of whom the eldest, thirteen-year-old Margaret, acted as a mother to her siblings and housekeeper to her father. The children slept in a closet attached to the larger room, and a hole in the wall allowed the girl, wise and old beyond her years, to witness everything that happened. During the next few weeks, as the only sober observer of proceedings, she was the one who could be relied on to help piece together a narrative of events on that fateful night.

The men who met to share a bottle or two of whisky that evening with Gallagher were fellow itinerant labourers, Teddy Keenan, Thomas Brannen, Andrew Finn, Mr Shield, William McHugh and Thomas Mooney. Keenan and Brannen had recently come from Ireland to Durham in search of work, and both had a reputation as tough men whom one crossed at one's own risk. Mooney's wife was serving a sentence in Northallerton Gaol at the time for some unspecified offence. Finn and Shield left the party quite early. In view of subsequent developments, it was just as well.

All had been on friendly terms when they entered the room, but before long quarrels broke out. It started when one of them, probably Keenan, made an offensive remark about Margaret, and Gallagher struck him. Further conflict arose when Keenan demanded a glass of whisky and Brannen, who had taken the bottle from Gallagher, would not give him any at first. Brannen was then persuaded to change his mind and grudgingly poured him half a glass, Keenan looked at it and angrily threw bottle and glass aside, breaking the latter against the wall. Both began arguing fiercely, and Mooney tried to pacify them.

When Keenan pushed Mooney down in his chair, he got up, sat on another, fell on the floor, cut his face and began bleeding. Margaret thought he had hurt himself on a sharp

Barnard Castle, c. 1850

edge or corner of the chair, and fetched some water from the outside tap to wash the wound. Keenan also sustained a cut above the eye, and Brannen stripped to the waist, eager to settle any argument with his fists. Both went outside but came back about ten minutes later. Neither seemed hurt, so they had probably settled their differences without resorting to a fight after all.

For what happened next, one has to rely on evidence from various other witnesses. Most of the men dispersed sometime during the small hours of 11 April. It was a clear, dry night, followed by a mild day, and if anything unusual was going on, somebody was bound to notice. Between 4 and 5 p.m. in the afternoon Thomas Dobson, an innkeeper at Bridgegate, was one of those who heard a rumour that a man was lying dead in the water. When he went to look he saw Ambrose White jumping in the water to try and rescue the body, and he went to give a hand. They found the dead man's coat was pulled part of the way over his head, and his hands were tightly clenched. After taking the body into a nearby yard, they went to inform the local doctor.

At about 7 p.m. McHugh and Gallagher came into Dobson's inn, arguing about a pocket handkerchief which McHugh claimed belonged to him. When Dobson referred to the body in the river and said he thought McHugh had some connection with it, the latter then denied that the handkerchief was his. Dobson then heard Gallagher mutter quietly to McHugh, 'Confess and hang Teddy [Keenan], and if thou does not hang Teddy, thou will be transported for life.'

McHugh then turned to Gallagher, saying, 'You don't mean to say that I did it?' 'Thou did the deed,' Gallagher answered, 'and I am speaking the truth the same as I am saying it.'

James Hannen, another labourer, said that on the same night he was in the Oddfellows Arms, Bridgegate, when McHugh came in and invited him to eat with him. When Hannen asked what he thought about the dead man in the river, which was evidently the talk of

Barnard Castle

the community by now, McHugh told him, 'I think nothing of it. He [Mooney] was dead before he got over the wall. I was in his company from half-past five till eleven o'clock that night.'

Dr John Mitchell was called in to see the body at Mooney's mother's house in Peel's Yard, Bridgegate, at about 4 p.m. on Sunday, to carry out a post-mortem. He discovered four wounds on the face, two on the right cheek, and two around the right eye. Those on the right cheek were not swollen, and must have been received either just before or just after death; neither penetrated through the thickness of the skin, and would not have proved fatal. If he had been strangled or suffocated, there would have been marks on his throat, and drowning was the most likely cause of death. The body contained a large quantity of gas, which explained why it had been floating when it was discovered, and appearances were consistent with the man having fallen into the river while drunk. An inquest on the afternoon of Tuesday 13 April at the Grey Horse Inn confirmed this finding, and proceedings were adjourned so that further enquiries might be made.

As yet, there was nothing to suggest that Mooney had been anything other than the victim of an unfortunate accident. Nevertheless the police decided that there was a case to answer and accordingly apprehended Gallagher, McHugh, Keenan and Brannen.

The adjourned enquiry was resumed at the Barnard Castle Police Station on 18 April. Margaret Gallagher, the first to give evidence, spoke of what she had seen of the comings and goings into her father's room. Various neighbours and tradesmen from Bridgegate testified to the unusual goings-on, especially George Walter, a tailor, who said that he had been in Dobson's inn on Sunday evening. The discovery of the body was being talked about, and Gallagher, who was among the present company, mentioned that on the previous night Mooney had been in his house drinking whisky. Walter said that if Mooney had been drunk, he might have gone down the yard and fallen down the steps into the river. When Gallagher said he did not go down the steps but went over the wall, by which time he was already dead, Walter said, 'I think you know something about it.' 'Oh, do I?' was Gallagher's retort, though he had made it obvious that he had some knowledge of the matter.

The case proceeded slowly, as the memories of those present were rather patchy. After another adjournment the hearing was resumed again at Witham Testimonial Hall, Barnard Castle, on 23 April. When the coroner summed up, the jury retired to announce that in their view there was no evidence to convict Brannen or Keenan, both of whom were released. There was, however, enough against Gallagher and McHugh to justify their being tried for the wilful murder of Mooney. Gallagher told the court that there were 'no two men in existence so innocently committed as we are at the present moment'.

They went on trial at Durham Assizes on 12 July under Mr Justice Archibald. Mr Skidmore and Mr Milvain were the counsel for the prosecution, while Mr Blackwell and Mr Ridley appeared for the defence.

Brannen, one of the first witnesses to be called, said that after he and Keenan had left the drinking party, they were walking to another friend's house and they saw three men standing several yards down the passage near Gallagher's house. Gallagher and McHugh were standing on either side of Mooney and both appeared to be supporting him by one arm. As they took him down the passage, he did not seem to be moving his legs. Keenan and Brannen followed them further at a distance and saw them take Mooney into a small yard adjoining Gallagher's house. When they got him as far as the wall, they lifted him up and laid him along the top. On the other side was the River Tees, and it was almost certain that any man in a drunken stupor who was pushed over would fall in and drown. McHugh then gave the command, 'Now!' 'My God Almighty, if I do,' was the horrified response of Gallagher, who had sobered up enough to realise that he was about to take part in killing a man. He repeated himself two or three times, so McHugh then took hold of Mooney with both hands and pushed him over. By this time Gallagher had moved away and was going back to his house. As he did so, McHugh shook his hand, saying, 'Nothing about this.'

At this point, the judge asked why Keenan and Brannen did not try and prevent Mooney from being thrown in, or at least try and save him by getting him out of the water. Brannen said he did not know what they were doing, but suspected they were up to no good, and he did not want to have anything to do with it. He continued to say that McHugh sat on the step of Patrick Finn's house, and Mrs Finn let him indoors at about 4.30 a.m. At about 10 a.m. that same day the Finns' daughter Winifred went to Gallagher's house on an errand and saw McHugh sitting inside. When he saw her, he growled, 'You can tell Teddy [Keenan] if I see him at opening time I will massacre him.' Gallagher was acquitted but censured for not doing more to prevent Mooney from being drowned, while McHugh was found guilty of murder. The jury deliberated for more than two hours, but the foreman made a strong recommendation for mercy on account of his previous good character. They considered that Gallagher had repented at the last moment and left McHugh to his own devices.

From the dock, McHugh said, 'All I have to say is that I will be cleared before God and man, and that I am as innocent of the charge as the child unborn; and it is very hard to be sentenced to death for a murder that Brannen and Teddy Keenan are guilty of. I am not frightened of it in my mind, nor should I regret meeting my end if it were not for my wife and children.'

He met his end on the gallows on 2 August 1875.

CHAPTER 15

'A VERY STEADY FELLOW'

Brandon, 1875

On the afternoon of 26 April 1875 twenty-one-year-old George Plummer went to meet his fiancée, eighteen-year-old Sarah Forster, from Chester Moor, intending to take her to his parents' house at Brandon for tea. Plummer worked in the mines at Brandon Colliery, a pit village three miles from Durham, while Forster's parents were licensees at the Clipper Inn. The young couple were due to be married on 3 May, exactly a week later, and at the weekend Plummer had completed arrangements at Durham Register Office for the ceremony at the Primitive Methodist chapel, New North Road, Durham. They had arranged that once they were married they would live with his mother until he had saved enough for them to buy a house of their own.

He had left Brandon Colliery on Saturday 24 April, going to Chester Moor to see her, and returning to work at the colliery on Monday morning. At 2 p.m. that afternoon she went to Durham with her parents where she met Plummer, who had also come to the city. After staying there a short while they went together to Brandon Colliery and his parents' home. On their way together they seemed to be on affectionate terms, as was only to be expected. She was heavily laden with various parcels, while he was carrying her wedding dress.

Sadly, she would never even wear the garment. As they arrived at the house they went into the parlour at the back part of the house, where they were alone. Barely a minute later Plummer's stepmother Mary Harding heard a loud report, ran into the room and found Sarah stretched on the floor in a pool of blood, shot through the head. Two balls had been fired, both of which had entered her mouth, one coming out at the back of her head, and the other below the jawbone. She had only had time to take off her gloves; her bonnet had fallen off her head towards her shoulder, she was fully clothed and there was no sign of any tampering with her clothing or any indication that a struggle might have taken place. Meanwhile Plummer had run away.

A horrified Mrs Harding fainted from shock, and when she came round she went to call on her neighbours for assistance, but they were out. Soon afterwards her husband Uriah returned, and he immediately called the police. Constable Kirkup rode into Durham and spoke to

Forest View, Brandon © Oliver Dixon

Superintendent Dunn, who immediately went to Brandon Colliery just in case Plummer had returned there. As there was no sign of him, police were sent out in all directions to search for him.

Meanwhile Kirkup went to the Forsters' house, followed by Dr Nairn of Brandon and Dr Stewart of Langley Moor. The latter had said that the shot or shots must have been fired into Sarah Forster's mouth, and presumably lodged in the spine or base of the skull, as there was no sign of them having left the body. There was a wound on the upper lip, but no other injury was visible, and an initial inspection in the room revealed no marks of a shot having lodged anywhere. It could not be conclusively established without a post-mortem whether one or two shots had been fired into the victim's mouth. Neighbours spoke of two shots, though the second could have been the echo of the first report. Plummer was known to have a revolver with six chambers, and it was assumed that after using it he must have taken it away with him.

An inquest was opened on 28 April and adjourned. The parents and sister of Sarah Forster, who were present in court, were all quite affected. By this time a second bullet had meanwhile been found embedded in the earth under the floor, which it had pierced.

For the prosecution, Superintendent Dunn said he was not prepared to continue with the case that day as they did not have sufficient evidence to proceed. All he could do at this stage was to call the doctor to give whatever relevant medical information he already had, after which he would ask the bench to remand the prisoner. In giving his assent, the chairman, the Revd H. D. Shafto, said in such a case it was impossible for them to do more than go step by step. Dr William Boyd, a practitioner in Durham, had just carried out a post-mortem on Sarah Forster, and described the wounds in some detail. Representing the

George Plummer shooting his fiancée Sarah Forster (Illustrated Police News)

prisoner, Mr Brignall asked when the case would be proceeded with. He doubted whether they would be able to call on many witnesses in the case and was surprised when Dunn said there would be at least twenty. The case was then postponed.

Meanwhile, Plummer was still at large. It was rumoured that he might have killed himself, but some people said they had seen him in other nearby mining villages. Once he had decided he would not be able to leave the area, he retraced his steps to Brandon, and everyone assumed that he would have gone to hide at his home. After the inquest was adjourned, Superintendent Dunn and his colleagues decided to surround the house. As they were about to do so they learned that another Brandon man, Thomas Green, was already keeping an eye on the place. He was rewarded when he saw the privy door open cautiously and a head furtively peep out before closing it again. Recognising Plummer instantly, he went and held the door firmly shut, as he told others to call the police. When they arrived the wanted man was captured and agreed to go quietly. He was handcuffed, searched, and two revolvers were taken out of his pockets before the police went with him to Durham Gaol.

On 4 May proceedings were resumed at Brancepeth Castle Inn, before Thomas Dunn, deputy coroner for Darlington Ward. Mary Harding said she did not know what became of Plummer after he killed Sarah Forster, and she did not see him again until he was found and taken into custody. After the pistol was discharged and she saw the girl was dead, she lifted her up then went to the back door, saw her husband coming, waited a few minutes and then fainted on the kitchen floor. When she told him what had happened, he went to seek the police. As soon as she called her next-door neighbour, a crowd rushed into the house. She found one pistol, which was produced in court, on the bed in the front room, and gave it to Inspector Bell that same evening. There was also a Dorringer pistol on the mantelpiece, also produced, where it was displayed as an ornament on the wall upstairs behind a piece of wood, so that nobody could get it. A friend wanted to take it away and keep it for the sake of her son, but she would not let him have it, and gave it to Inspector Bell on Wednesday. A third pistol, also produced, was found under the cushion of the sofa in the front room and she hid it in the closet between the wood and the wall, where it remained until Wednesday when she told her husband to give it to the Inspector.

A few hours after the shooting, she saw Inspector Bell search Plummer's bedroom and box. To Mr Brignall she admitted that she knew her son had three pistols, and two revolvers of five and six chambers each. Since boyhood he had been obsessed with firearms, and often amused himself by firing at any target that came to hand. At school he was 'always fond of little cannons and gunpowder'. He had been 'in a weak state' since the age of sixteen, which she put down to his having grown very fast; between sixteen and seventeen he grew five inches in one year. Two Christmases ago he had been unwell, and took fourteen weeks off work. 'He was very low in his mind, and was a very light sleeper' and had been under the care of several doctors.

He and Sarah Forster had been together since July 1874, and they had planned to marry earlier but postponed the ceremony because he was ill. She approved of the match, and had never once heard them quarrel. He was 'a very steady fellow, and has been a Good Templar; he has only taken wine and spirits for his health since he joined the order'.

Next in the witness box was Joseph, Sarah's father. The last time he had seen her alive was at about 12.50 on the day of her death, in his own house. She was getting ready to take the 2.12 train at Plawsworth for Durham, when they arranged that he would meet her at Plawsworth Station off the 7.39 train that evening. On the night of Saturday 24 April Plummer had come to their house, leaving twenty-four hours later. Questioned by Mr Brignall as to the young man's personality he said that Plummer tended to be rather moody and not inclined to be lively or communicative, though he had been very pleasant that Sunday afternoon.

Other witnesses giving evidence included Ann Humble, of Queen Street, Brandon Colliery, who had helped to lay out the dead body of Sarah Forster. Earlier that afternoon she had seen the couple walking towards the house, Sarah laughing and joking as if she had not a care in the world. Uriah Harding, Plummer's stepfather, who had been married to his mother for fourteen years, told how he had returned home to find his wife on the floor 'in a swooning kind of way', went into the front room and found Sarah's body, then went to alert the police. The young man had been ill off and on for about eighteen months, and some of the doctors said they thought he was consumptive.

After further evidence from other members of the police force, surgeons Boyd and Stewart, and others, the coroner summed up, and it only took the jury a few minutes to return a verdict of 'guilty of wilful murder'. In his absence, Plummer was committed to take his trial at the next assizes.

At a special sitting of the Durham County Police Court, Plummer was brought up on remand to answer the charge. He sat on a chair throughout the proceedings, sitting very still and seldom raising his eyes from the floor. Most of the evidence had already been heard at the inquest, but one new, potentially disturbing piece of information was given by Henry Hamilton, husband of Isabella, sister of the deceased. On 21 April, he said that Sarah Forster had been in his house and later Plummer had arrived. Before supper, as he was standing before the fire he took a newspaper, the *London Clipper*, from his pocket. Showing it to Sarah, he pointed out something to her, to which she said, 'There is a lot of you for such like'. The object of their attention was a picture in the paper. Elizabeth Forster then took up the story on behalf of her sister Isabella Hamilton, who was too ill to attend court, as she described the picture — of a young man cutting his sweetheart's throat and then killing himself. Everyone in court was horrified.

Plummer was formally charged, and when asked if he had anything to say, shook his head. The chairman committed him to appear at the next session of Durham Summer Assizes, where the trial opened on 9 July before Mr Justice Archibald, with Messrs Edge and Sowerby for the prosecution and Messrs Wright and Jones for the defence. The deathly pale prisoner was provided with a chair, and throughout the hearing he looked down at the ground with a fixed expression. When charged with murder, at first he gave no sign that he had heard. After he was asked repeatedly, he shook his head and muttered indistinctly, 'not guilty'. Once the evidence at previous hearings was recapitulated, much was made of the prisoner's ill-health, giddiness, low spirits and poor appetite.

Mrs Harding confirmed that in her opinion he had deteriorated in the last year. His memory was becoming worse, he tended to hesitate in speech, and while he was talking he tended to forget what he wanted to say, especially names and places. Much was also made of his obsession with weapons, in particular regular purchases of guns since he was sixteen years old, and his ownership of a dagger. The surgeon William Boyd suggested that he was probably not insane, but more likely an imbecile; 'he was in a state of mind to know the nature of such an act and its consequences'.

On the second day of the trial Francis Ford, Plummer's uncle, a miner from Hetton, mentioned a walk they had recently taken together. At the time Plummer had a loaded pistol in one of his pockets, half-cocked it, pointed it to his own temples with a smile, and said, 'Eh?' On another occasion Plummer said to him that he often talked about his illness, saying, 'I wish I were dead, and then I would be out of the road.'

In summing up, the judge said that it was for the jury to decide whether the defence were right in suggesting that he was not in a state of mind in which he would be responsible for his actions. There could be no doubt that he had committed the murder, and as two shots were fired it could not be thought accidental. After retiring for one hour and twenty minutes, the jury returned a verdict of 'not guilty' on the grounds of insanity. The judge ordered him to be detained during Her Majesty's pleasure, and on behalf of the defence Mr Wright asked that any pistols and money found on him should be handed over to his friends.

CHAPTER 16

THE IRISH AFFRAY AT WEST HARTLEPOOL

West Hartlepool, 1875

On 12 June 1875 members of the Irish community were at the centre of a riot at the Waverley Hotel, on the edge of West Hartlepool. Nobody was killed, but the authorities saw fit to hold a major enquiry before the magistrates four days later.

Nine men were charged jointly with assaulting a fellow Irishman, Owen Morgan, and Mr Young, landlord of the Waverley Hotel. Five of them were also charged with assault on Police Constable Pudney and four with a similar offence against Police Constable Clarke, at the same time and place. All nine were additionally charged with drunken and riotous conduct on the same occasion and wilful damage to the Waverley Hotel.

Between 7 and 8 p.m. on the evening of 12 June, Morgan had been standing at the bar of the hotel, when two of the prisoners, Peter Carr and Michael McDonough, walked in. A couple of minutes later the house was besieged with a mob of about fifty other men, about thirty of whom forced their way into the bar and made a rush for Morgan, knocking him to the floor and kicking him as he lay. The barman immediately called Mr Young, who armed himself with a staff and tried to protect Morgan. After being treated very roughly himself, Young managed to clear the assailants from the bar and send them outside.

As they reached the door three of them, Carr, James Fitzstephen and Peter Maughan, attacked Young and beat him with their belts, while the others hurled stones and slag at him as well as at the windows, several of which were smashed. Constables Pudney and Clarke then arrived on the scene, but were knocked down and severely kicked and beaten. If Young had not succeeded in defending the door with his staff, while a man inside dragged the policemen indoors, they would probably have been killed. Clarke was covered in blood and lost consciousness for a while.

Sergeant Wilkinson, who assisted Sergeant Alderson and other constables in apprehending the prisoners, told the court that at one point he met the mob, and several others who were not under arrest, marching four abreast under the leadership of Matthew Green. It

Church Street, West Hartlepool, c. 1900

was the latter who gave his men 'the word of command' and defied the officer when he requested them peacefully to disband.

For the defence, Mr Skidmore called a witness to prove an alibi on behalf of two of the prisoners, John Hanley and Patrick Swift. He then asked for the prisoners Peter Maughan, William Feeney and Carr to be sworn for a similar purpose, but their evidence proved to be unsatisfactory.

After retiring for fifteen minutes to consider the case, the bench said they had decided that all nine were guilty of assaulting Morgan. All were sentenced to one month's imprisonment with hard labour, and a similar additional term for the attack on Young. McDonough, Fitzstephen, Carr and Hanley were given a further two months' hard labour for the assault on Constable Pudney, and McDonough, Swift, Carr and Hanley another two months for that on Constable Clark. In addition to these sentences, which would run concurrently, each man was required to pay 40s damages and costs for the acts of wilful damage, with the alternative of an additional fourteen days' hard labour.

Green was then charged with inciting the prisoners to commit the assaults. He was fined an extra £20, or two months' hard labour in default.

CHAPTER 17

'A VERY MITIGATED KIND OF MANSLAUGHTER'

Darlington, 1875

Thomas Snowdon, an engineer aged twenty-five, lived in London. On 25 September 1875 he came to stay with his brother-in-law, Robert Hall, a veterinary surgeon, at his house in Darlington. He left two days later on the 9.20 train from town, and was not seen afterwards until brought into Hall's house by the police, suffering from head injuries and a nosebleed. As he was fully conscious, Hall asked him how he was and he answered he felt quite satisfactory, though he did not say how he had been hurt. However, he soon took a turn for the worse and died at 5 a.m. two days later.

The events of 27 September leading up to his death were later recalled in court by Thomas Hunton, a roper. He had been standing at the corner of High Street, smoking his pipe, when Henry Walker, a friend of his, came up to him and asked for a bit of tobacco, but he had none to give him. He shook hands with him several times, but as he was obviously the worse for drink, Hunton told him to go home. Just then Thomas Snowdon, on his own, came along and stopped in front of them. Walker asked him for a chew of tobacco and Snowdon gave him a small piece. That would not do, Walker said, 'Give us a bit more, that's not plenty'.

Snowdon refused to give him any more, but gesticulated wildly as he boasted of what he could do to a man and how he knew how to box. Though he did not actually threaten Walker, while he was talking he accidentally hit him with the back of his hand in the face. An angry Walker told him he deserved 'a damned good thumping for that', and before the situation got out of control, Hunton advised them both to go home.

Walker then struck Snowdon in the face with his fist, knocking him backwards over on to the pavement, and ran away. Another man was standing nearly fifty yards away and Hunton walked over to him, asking for assistance. He saw Snowdon was lying insensible so he went over to help, and almost at once a crowd gathered on the spot to help lift the injured man up as he was bleeding heavily from the nose. It was clear that Walker and Snowdon were both equally drunk and threatening to get aggressive with each other.

When a policeman, Sergeant Gould, arrived on the scene, he led Snowdon, who was back on his feet and seemed to have recovered, away for his own safety.

An inquest was held on 30 September with the coroner, John Settle. Gould said that at about 11.15 on Monday night he saw a girl run for a policeman to Cattaneon's Corner, and saw there was something wrong. There were several gentlemen holding Snowdon up, and managed to stop his nose from bleeding. He had him taken to Mr Hall's house in St John's Road after finding out who he was. On the way there Snowdon put his hand up to his head, said it felt sore and that he must have had a fall. Although still smelling of alcohol and covered with blood, he walked home without any difficulty. Enquiries were made, and it appeared that Walker had struck Snowdon. After the latter suddenly died, Sergeant Edgar took Walker into custody, and he was remanded by the magistrates. Snowdon said he had had a 'bat' in the face, but he did not know his attacker.

Dr Tarleton said he was summoned by Mr Hall, shortly after 9 a.m., to see the deceased and found him in an unconscious state. Only one lung was still functioning, and he said Snowdon had received a serious injury. He last saw Snowdon alive, but unconscious and sinking, just before 11 p.m. that night. Dr Foss was also there all evening, and the previous day he had attended a post-mortem. He said Snowdon died from concussion of the brain, resulting from a fracture of the skull caused by a fall or blow from a heavy instrument. Foss was present with Dr Tarleton at the time and agreed with his evidence.

When recalled, Hall said that when Snowdon was taken to his house he immediately asked him if he was any worse. 'No, not much,' was the reply. He sat down on the stairs to take off his boots. Hall noticed that he had stopped bleeding, examined his head and found a slight abrasion, which he felt did not give cause for concern. Snowdon then followed Hall upstairs, undressed and got ready for bed, sleeping in a room immediately above Hall's. About an hour after Hall left him, he heard him tumble out of bed. Going up to check, he found Snowdon lying on his side between the bed and the door. Apart from having had a minor nosebleed he seemed to be all right, and Hall asked him to get up. Snowdon indistinctly muttered something which sounded like he would rather be left alone where he was. Hall tried to lift him up, but found he was too heavy, so he decided to try and make him a bed on the floor, as he thought it would be safer. He checked Snowdon's pulse, which was a little quicker than before, but he hoped he would be better after a good night's sleep. All the same, he went to keep an eye on Snowdon at intervals during the night, occasionally waking him, as he was still tossing a good deal.

In the morning Snowdon's pulse was much faster. Hall sent for the doctor, told Snowdon to get out of bed and persuaded him to take a drink, but Snowdon was very lethargic and murmured feebly that he only wanted to stay quietly in bed.

Dr Tarleton said he was sure that the fracture of the skull had occurred when Snowdon fell down in the street. Hall's evidence of a fall from the bed would have exacerbated the bleeding, but it was unlikely to have contributed to his death. It was also probably relevant, said the doctor, that although the deceased generally enjoyed good health, at the age of twelve he had sustained a severe head injury after falling from a pony.

The inquest jury passed a verdict of manslaughter against Henry Walker, and he was charged by the police court with causing Snowdon's death. On 4 March he went on trial at Durham Assizes under Mr Justice Mellor, with Mr Ridley prosecuting and Mr Skidmore defending. Under cross-examination by Mr Skidmore, Hall said that Snowdon fell heavily out of bed, and the floors were wooden, not covered with carpet. Snowdon had not been very steady on his feet and was inclined to be quarrelsome when drunk. Thomas Hunton said that when the deceased struck Walker, the latter said, 'You want me for that'. Gould and Tarleton also repeated the evidence given at the inquest.

The judge summed it up as a very painful case, 'but a very mitigated kind of manslaughter'. The counsel for the defence had seen he could not struggle against the evidence to try and get a verdict for the prisoner, and the jury found him 'not guilty'. 'Not guilty,' said the judge. 'That is your verdict, not mine. In point of law, I believe there is no doubt about it that the prisoner is guilty. You are, however, quite the masters of the situation, and therefore if you choose, you can find him not guilty.' Turning to Walker, he told him that he was discharged. 'Certainly, if the jury had found you guilty, you would have had a very light sentence indeed. They have taken the law very much into their own hands. However, you may be discharged. No great injustice has been done.'

Skidmore said he could not possibly have resisted the evidence.

'You are quite right, Mr Skidmore,' said the judge, 'you have pleaded most successfully.' At this there was laughter in court. He said the jury had reached their verdict after taking into account the provocation received by the prisoner. In his view it was not a matter of very great importance, as he would only have had about a week's imprisonment.

CHAPTER 18

ON THE STREETS OF SHOTTON

Shotton, 1876

A few ill-tempered exchanges and arguments at Shotton one winter afternoon soon got out of hand and resulted in a manslaughter charge. On 5 February 1876 James Potts and James Tate went to the Bee Hive Inn at about 2 p.m. for a drink together. As they were standing at the bar they saw two men whom Potts did not recognise. One asked him merely if he could spell a word, and Potts told him with a grin that he could spell more words than the man who was talking to him. The other man turned round and hit out at him, and the landlord had to order them outside.

As they reached the door, both men set on Potts, who immediately took to his heels. They were too fast for him, easily overtook him, and they had another fight outside the Albert Inn. A third party then struck Potts and knocked him over, after which five or six men whom he later claimed were Irish began kicking him, with shouts of 'Kill the bastard'. He did not know whether Samuel Donley was among them. However, he recognised James Tate, an acquaintance, to whom he called to help him get back on his feet. Potts did not give his attackers a second chance, but begged them to leave him alone as he did not want any mischief. He took himself home at once and went to bed to recover from the shock.

This was only the start of much aggression in the town that afternoon. At about the same time William Dow, a labourer at Shotton, saw James Tate and Samuel Donley standing together. Tate was striking at a reluctant Donley, who said he did not want to fight. A boy was holding on to Tate and trying to restrain him, but he broke free, stooped down, picked up a brick, and threw it at Donley, who was walking away at the time. The brick struck Donley and knocked him down and he lay stunned for several minutes, before someone helped him to his feet. Dow then went to look for a policeman, but without success.

An inquest was held at the Commercial Inn, Shotton Colliery, on 15 February. Donley's body was identified by his wife, Catherine. She said that after he had returned to the house, her twenty-nine-year-old husband never went out again. The last time he ever came downstairs was two days after the attack, but after that he returned to bed and died of his injuries early on the afternoon of 13 February.

There was no shortage of witnesses who had been around in the village that afternoon to describe some of the exchanges that had ensued. The first to be called was Elizabeth Miller, wife of the keeper of the Red Brick Inn. She said she saw Donley standing at the corner, and noticed Tate trying to strike him as he backed towards the shop. As she had only been watching them for about a minute, and she not see any further fighting or quarrelling.

Henry Wilkinson, an assistant in Mr Atkinson's corner shop, said he had heard a disturbance outside the shop on 5 February. He looked out and saw Tate standing in front of Donley, squaring at him, while Donley was parrying Tate's blows and retreating. When Donley came near the shop windows, Wilkinson pushed him off into the channel. Tate fell on his hands and knees, and on getting up again he picked up a brick and struck Donley on the head. Donley fell to the ground.

Patrick Ward said he came to Mr Atkinson's shop, and on coming out he saw Donley backing down the street, and Tate 'making buts' at him. Tate went and picked up a half brick. When he was two or three yards from Donley, he flung the brick at him, striking him on the head and knocking him down. This was corroborated by George Raffarty, a fireman, who also came out of the shop at about the same time.

Robert Bradley, a local miner, said he picked Donley up, and told Tate he had killed him. Tate looked at Donley, bit his lip, turned very pale and walked away without a word.

George Dunscombe, assistant to Dr Wilson, saw Donley at about 3.30 in the afternoon at his own house. He was unconscious, bleeding from the skull, and had sustained several bone fractures. Dunscombe prescribed carbolic acid lotion and other remedies, and Donley came round on Sunday afternoon. He continued in a semi-conscious state until Wednesday, when Dr Wilson was sent for, but went into a coma on Thursday and died on Sunday afternoon. Dunscombe was certain that the injuries to the head must have been caused by a blow either from a blunt instrument or a stone. He had tried to visit Donley again on Saturday evening but could not as the house was locked and nobody was with him.

Dr Wilson gave similar evidence, saying he had seen Donley on Wednesday and realised the skull was fractured. He did a post-mortem twenty-four hours after death and found the only external mark of violence was the injury to the head. The internal organs of the chest were healthy, though the coats of the stomach were slightly diseased, most likely from hard living. A close examination of the skull showed that the brain and its coverings corresponding with the external wound were ruptured, pieces of the bone had penetrated the brain and an abscess was forming at the seat of the fracture, the cause of death. In his opinion, Donley must have been standing when he was struck with the blow which proved fatal, as the fractures would have been very light if he was running away at the time.

Samuel Pickard, the deputy overman, said he saw the fight going on at about 2.30 p.m., with Potts on the ground and several men kicking him, including Donley who kicked him once, and noticed Potts calling to Tate for assistance. Tate never denied having thrown a brick in self-defence. Joseph Noble, a grocer whose shop overlooked the scene, went out of his shop to close the windows as the row was becoming so noisy.

Police Constable Machin apprehended Tate on 7 February and charged him with cutting and wounding Donley. Tate admitted that he did throw a brick, but four or five men were kicking him and Potts at the time. On 10 February Donley was close to death, and Machin apprehended him a second time.

After all the witnesses had given evidence, the jury retired for a short time and returned a verdict of manslaughter, and Tate was accordingly committed to the next assizes. In conclusion, Mr G. H. Taylor, the jury foreman, said they would like to make a complaint to be laid before the chief constable or the magistrates. The jury considered there should be a policeman in the colliery villages on pay Saturdays. Every policeman had been taken to the court in Castle Eden on the Saturday in question. Had an officer been present in the village, this incident would almost certainly never have happened. The coroner fully agreed with their recommendation and promised to bring it to the attention of the chairman of the Castle Eden Petty Sessions. These extreme cases had occurred since the court day had been changed to the pay Saturday.

The case came to trial at Durham Assizes before Mr Justice Miller on 1 March 1876, with Mr Ridley and Mr Granger conducting the case for the prosecution and Mr Blackwell for the defence.

Martin Maloney, a miner of Shotton, said that on that day he was in Albert Terrace between 3 and 4 p.m. and saw a row taking place between several men, and the prisoner was among them. Potts was knocked down there. The prisoner had a coal rake in his hand but was not using it, and Donley was not there at the time. Elizabeth Miller, Henry Wilkinson, Patrick Ward, George Raffarty, and Robert Bradley were also called to repeat the evidence they had given at the inquest.

Mr Blackwell withdrew a plea of 'not guilty', and the judge told him he had exercised wise discretion. There was clear proof of manslaughter, and the prisoner had admitted to the constable that he had thrown the brick. He said in mitigation that he did not look on it as so aggravated a case as he should have done had there been no provocation. The jury likewise took little time to agree on a manslaughter verdict. It then emerged that Tate had something of a reputation, having been fined seventeen times for petty offences since 1870, and under the circumstances it would not be possible to pass an unduly lenient sentence. He was given fourteen months with hard labour.

CHAPTER 19

MATRICIDE AND ATTEMPTED SUICIDE

Coxhoe, 1876

William and Sarah Heathwaite lived at Coxhoe with their baby son Thomas. It was an unhappy marriage, and early on the morning of 29 February 1876 they had one furious argument too many. She decided she could take no more. At about 8 a.m. she picked up the baby, then aged four and a half months, walked out of the house and went in the direction of her mother's house at Quarrington Hill. Sadly, she did not go straight there, but instead she climbed the rails around Crow Trees Reservoir and threw herself and the child into the icy waters.

Coxhoe

Mr Roe, walking past at the time, heard a woman's voice calling out in distress. Looking over the edge, it took him a while before he could see her body floating on the surface, and when he pulled her out she was unconscious. Another ninety minutes elapsed before the tiny body of Thomas was recovered, but by then he was dead. Roe went for a doctor, and Dr Blandford gave her artificial respiration and then took her to her mother's house. The police were contacted, and she remained on the premises, weak and exhausted, for the rest of the day under surveillance.

Next day she was taken to the Court House, Durham, and brought before Mr E. J. Meynell. He charged her with the wilful murder of her son, and she was remanded in custody. At an inquest the following day at Oak Tree Inn, Quarrington Hill, the jury were out for two and a quarter hours before returning a verdict of manslaughter. In their view she had thrown herself and her child into the water while acting under momentary impulse.

The case was heard at Durham Summer Assizes before Mr Justice Lush on 1 July. Mr Skidmore was counsel for the prosecution, but as the Grand Jury had found neither a bill for murder or manslaughter, he did not propose to offer any evidence on the coroner's committal, and said they would accept an acquittal for her. With this the judge agreed. Sarah Heathwaite was placed in the dock, but pleaded 'not guilty'. Mr Justice Lush said that everyone had chosen to regard the matter as an accident. There would be no evidence against her, and she was discharged.

CHAPTER 20

'I'LL LEARN YOU TO STAY OUT'

Stockton, 1876

John Pattison of 6 Hardwick Terrace, Stockton, a painter by trade, was an extremely strict Victorian paterfamilias, not to be crossed. It was a lesson that his sixteen-year-old Georgiana learnt too late.

On the morning of 13 May 1876, Georgiana met her widowed aunt Annie Sophia Trotter in High Street while they were both out shopping. Mrs Trotter, who had long been like a second mother to her niece, was going to the market for vegetables and the girl to the butcher's. They chatted for a few minutes before going their separate ways. That evening Georgiana went to her house for some coals, as she did regularly. Soon after 11 p.m. her father followed her there in an ugly temper, ordering her home with threats if she did not come immediately. At the time Mrs Trotter, Walter McNeal, her lodger, and Thomas Pollard, a friend, were standing together in the yard behind Mrs Trotter's house. Calling him to one side, Mrs Trotter told him she did not like to give him the coals before the stranger, Mr Pollard, if he was going to be unpleasant. McNeal turned away without a word down the kitchen stairs, where Georgiana and Selina Sarah Trotter, her sister-in-law, were getting the coals. While she was at the top of the kitchen stairs, she heard John Pattison say to his daughter, 'If you are not out of this house, and sharp, I'll lift you.'

Georgiana obediently followed him out of the house, carrying the coals in a pail, and on arriving home laid down on the sofa.

Mrs Trotter and her sister-in-law Selina had a feeling that the girl was going to get a thrashing once she was home, and they thought that if they followed father and daughter there he would probably not dare to do such a thing. Going to the back of the house, they stood outside and looked through the kitchen window where the blind was short enough for them to see and hear what was going on. Pattison was sitting on a sofa, and they watched him get up, go to the middle of the floor, and heard him tell his daughter brusquely to get up at once. He spoke to her three times, and on each occasion she cried out as if she was afraid. Annie Trotter then knocked at the back door, and told him that if she heard any more noise, she would go straight to the police.

He sent Georgiana's stepmother to see Annie Trotter, and ask her to go indoors but not say anything. Mrs Trotter said she would on condition that if she found any reason to speak out, she could hardly be expected to keep quiet. 'Most assuredly you don't come in here if you won't hold your tongue,' Mrs Pattison snapped, slamming the door in her face. The Trotters stood outside for a while just in case the girl was about to come to any harm, but they heard no noise and assumed all must be well. After about fifteen minutes, they noticed the gas in the kitchen being turned down very low, and ten minutes later it was turned full on again. At the same time the Pattisons also put something, probably a thick cloth, across the bottom of the window while the gas was low, to stop spectators from seeing in. The Trotters stood keeping watch there until about 1 a.m., when the gas was put out, and they went home, hoping for the best. They were not to know that neither of them would ever see Georgiana alive again.

By the time Mr Pattison came downstairs on Sunday morning Georgiana was back on the sofa, badly beaten. Soon afterwards the police received reports of a death at 6 Albert Terrace, Stockton. On arriving there they found they had been given the wrong address, and despite making extensive enquiries, it was not until Monday morning that they found out it was 6 Hardwick Terrace instead.

A post-mortem was held that same afternoon, and immediately afterwards Inspector Bell arrested Pattison on suspicion of causing his daughter's death. Meanwhile John Settle, the coroner, opened an inquest at the police court. Mrs Trotter, the first witness called, described how she had been with Georgiana on Saturday morning and again in the evening. When they met in town while shopping, she was in her usual high spirits and did not appear concerned about anything. Replying to questions from the jury and coroner about the evening's events, she said she and her sister-in-law were outside at the back of the house for about an hour and a half. They had not heard any rows before, but Georgiana had complained to her of having been severely beaten by her father on previous occasions, though her stepmother always treated her kindly. Mr Pattison, said Mrs Trotter, was 'a steady man, but the most violent-tempered man I ever knew'. Even when sober, he had a formidable temper and his family feared he might turn violent. Georgiana was a 'steady, respectable girl' and had certainly had nothing to drink. Mr Pattison did not generally object to his daughter visiting Mrs Trotter's house, and when he ordered her home Georgiana was not in the habit of answering back. Mrs Trotter had never known her to be uncivil to anyone, least of all the father of whom she was so afraid.

The second witness was her sister-in-law (and Mrs Pattison's sister) Selina Trotter, of 1 Havelock Terrace. She said she had gone to Annie's house at about 11 p.m. and found Mr Pattison standing on the back door step. His daughter was downstairs in the coal house, and Selina went down to her as she was getting coals into a pan. Her father came down after her into the kitchen, and said that if she did not go soon, he would 'lift her out'. Selina advised Georgiana to go, and she would get the coals herself. As the girl was always so frightened of him, both Mrs Trotters went after them to No. 6 to keep an eye on the situation.

Stockton, c. 1900

Selina's brother Fenwick, who lodged with the Pattisons, came to see her just after 8 a.m. on Sunday. Evidently trying to break the tragic news gently, at first he asked her to go to the Pattisons' house as Georgiana had been taken ill. She said she would come shortly — and then he told her that the girl was dead. When she arrived at the house she saw the body laid out on the kitchen floor, with her lifeless hand on her father's knee as he sat sobbing beside her, while her stepmother apparently looked quite unaffected. There were no immediately visible marks on Georgiana's body, except on her forehead, and no traces of blood. When she asked Mrs Pattison how the girl had died, the answer was a defensive retort that her father had never touched her.

When questioned by Inspector Bell and the jury, Selina said Georgiana had often complained to her of physical and mental abuse from her father, and had shown her marks on her legs, caused by him kicking her. Selina added that she had seen him thrash his daughter, and he was always ready to correct or even scold her on the most trifling matters.

Fenwick Trotter said that at about midnight on Saturday, he was sitting in the Pattisons' kitchen reading, when he heard a rap at the door. He knew John had gone to look for his daughter, and although he knew she had gone on a perfectly respectable errand to the Trotters' house, he was in 'a great passion' about her staying out so late. As the door opened she came in and fell on the floor. Her father was standing two yards away from her, with a broom (produced in court) in his hand. After she had collapsed, he said, 'I'll learn you to stay out.'

Mrs Pattison had gone to bed, but came downstairs on hearing the disturbance, and Georgiana was still on the floor. Meanwhile Fenwick heard Annie Trotter come to the back door, but could not hear what she was saying. After Selina came in, he asked Georgiana if she was hurt and she complained that her head was aching. He then went to bed, leaving her sitting on the floor while her father and stepmother were with her. Though he had seen John strike her before, he said, she deserved it, as she was self-willed and obstinate. This time he did not see John hit her or kick her, or hear him order her to get up, but he knew she was getting a scolding for being out late. She never spoke, merely cried out when she fell, at which point he turned round and went to her, when she moved into a sitting position. When she did not try to get up on her feet, he made no effort to help her up.

'You must have been accustomed to that sort of thing, not to take any notice of it, or assist her,' remarked one of the jurymen. When asked by the coroner, he said her father did not help her up either. The inquest was then adjourned until 7 p.m.

Meanwhile, on the afternoon of 16 May, the prisoner was brought up before magistrates on a charge of causing his daughter's death. Superintendent Booth stated the nature of the charge, proposing only to submit sufficient evidence to justify his being remanded, as the coroner's inquest was still pending. Fenwick Trotter repeated the evidence already given to the coroner, and Pattison was then remanded until Thursday next.

When the inquest resumed under Mr Settle and the jury, Mr Trotter was recalled to continue his evidence. He said he did not know where Georgiana was from 1.00 to 8.00 on Sunday morning, as she usually slept on the sofa in the kitchen. She was not in the habit of staying out late, except when she had been sent on an errand, and he did not understand what her father had meant when he threatened to 'lift' her. To the jury, he said he did not know when she left the house on Saturday night. He was not in the kitchen when the gas was turned down or when there was an additional blind put up. Mrs Pattison came downstairs and merely asked what the matter was. Georgiana was then on the floor, and her father was standing at the end of the table. Fenwick Trotter did not see him hit her at all or hear any more disturbance that night. He slept alone in the bedroom upstairs, and never heard John Pattison and his wife go to bed, though their bedroom was below his. When John came downstairs in the morning, said Fenwick, he cursed his wife soundly, even though she could hardly have been held responsible for what had happened. As Georgiana was plainly very ill, Mrs Pattison called Fenwick at about 7.45 a.m. Though it might have been more appropriate if the girl's stepmother had gone to call the doctor herself, Fenwick went to do so and then tell his sister. There had not been any conversation between him and Mr and Mrs Pattison on the subject of Georgiana or what might have happened to her.

The next witness, Walter McNeal, an engineer's apprentice who lodged with Mrs Trotter, was at her house when Georgiana arrived on Saturday night at about 11 p.m., and he did not know why she was there. As he was standing behind the door when her father came in hurriedly and pushed it open violently, he assumed that she must have done something wrong for him to be in such a state. McNeal asked who was there and Pattison did not answer, merely asking, 'Where's Georgiana?' He then saw her, and told her to go home at once. She went downstairs, followed by her father and McNeal behind them, as he heard Pattison say, 'If you are not out quick I will lift you out quick'. McNeal saw him go upstairs after that, and then out of the house, but did not notice Georgiana leave as he went upstairs.

David Hope Watson, a medical practitioner from Stockton, said he had an urgent message on Sunday soon after 8 a.m. from Fenwick Trotter to go to the Pattisons' house as his daughter was dying. He dressed quickly, went out and met a messenger begging him to hurry. Mr Pattison was sitting on the kitchen floor when he arrived, supporting his daughter in his arms, and he asked Watson if he thought she was alive. Watson could feel no pulse; he examined her and told her father that she was dead. Both parents began to cry bitterly and asked him if he could bring her back to life.

When Watson asked what had caused the marks on her brow and nose, Mr Pattison pointed out her bed on the sofa, and said she must have got them by falling off the sofa in her nightgown. The doctor said that 'would hardly do' for him and there would have to be an inquest. Mr Pattison dreaded that and asked if they could possibly do without one, but Watson said he could not issue a death certificate under such circumstances. Asked what should be done, Watson told him to report a sudden death to the police and they would do the rest. He told them to lay out the body, and it would be examined in due course.

At the post-mortem on Monday, he was assisted by Dr Mackenzie and Dr Bain. They found the body well-nourished and in good condition, with a bruise on the forehead, extending downwards over the nose, and a slight abrasion of skin over the nose. The skull was fractured from ear to ear, and a circular piece was detached and split in various directions. Here Watson passed the skull round for the jury to inspect. There was blood on the surface of the brain, from a ruptured blood vessel, but the brain and the body's other organs were otherwise healthy. Death had resulted from a fractured skull after a severe blow, probably from the broom. The jury asked him if the deceased's falling over backwards or forwards might have caused the injury, but he said this was most unlikely. Answering a question from Inspector Bell of Stockton Police, he said a person injured as badly as that would almost certainly be unable get up and walk across a room unaided.

On behalf of the local police, Bell said that after the incident had been reported to them at the station early on Monday morning, he and Detective Sergeant Heslop arrived at No. 6 Havelock Terrace about 9 a.m., saw Pattison and asked who had died. He said it was his daughter and gave her name. Bell asked for particulars about her death, and was told:

She was coming into the house with some coals, on Saturday night, and when she got into the room she fell. I went to her and asked if she was hurt, and she then complained of her back. She then got up, put off her clothes, laid down on the sofa, and said she wanted to go to sleep.

Next morning, when he got up at 8 a.m., he found her lying on the floor close to death and sent for the doctor at once, but it was too late. Bell went upstairs, looked at the body, noticed some marks on the nose and forehead, then came down and asked Pattison how he thought she had got them. He said she must have fallen off the sofa during the night. At 4.30 p.m. the following day he took Pattison into custody, brought him to the police station, and said he was going to lock him up on suspicion of causing the death of his daughter. To this Pattison made no reply. After putting him in the cell, Bell made further enquiries, and three hours later charged Pattison with wilful murder. Pattison shook his head, murmuring, 'No, no, no'.

Detective Sergeant Heslop, also of Durham County Police, Stockton, said that on Monday morning he went to the house and found the broom in the pantry. He showed it to the witness, Fenwick Trotter, who confirmed it was the same one Pattison had in his hand on Saturday night.

The jury returned a verdict of wilful murder against John Pattison, who was committed for trial. They also reprimanded Fenwick Trotter for doing nothing to help or protect the girl.

On Wednesday 18 May Pattison was committed for manslaughter at Stockton Borough Police Court. The police were represented by Superintendent Booth and Inspector Bell, while the prisoner was represented by Mr W. R. Fawcett. The slightly-built, dejected-looking Pattison looked so weak that he was allowed to remain seated in the dock.

Anne and Selina Trotter both repeated the evidence they had given at the inquest. When cross-examined by Mr Fawcett, they confirmed that on Saturday night the prisoner had been sober; he was 'a sober and respectable man'. Dr Watson said that as the cause of death was a fracture of the skull, considerable violence must have been inflicted, and it was almost certainly through being hit with the brush. The marks on Georgiana Pattison's forehead, nose and right hip might have been explained by a fall from the sofa.

Pattison was charged by the clerk with feloniously killing his daughter, and he was cautioned in the usual way. At the trial at Durham Assizes on 5 July before Mr Justice Denman, he pleaded guilty to manslaughter. Although none of the witnesses except Fenwick Trotter had made any such suggestion, the judge seemed to think that Georgiana Pattison had somehow brought her fate on herself. To the impartial observer, she had basically done nothing wrong but inadvertently get on the wrong side of an unduly irascible parent. Nevertheless, in his summing up, Denman said he had seriously considered everything he had heard and what was said in the prisoner's favour by the witnesses that were called against him.

You were a sober, honest man, a good husband, and a good father. You, unfortunately, were the means of causing the death of your daughter. As I have said before, you had very great cause to be angry with her. She had provoked you very much, and done things that would make you very anxious; and I am quite certain that when you struck her, under considerable provocation, you had no idea what the consequences would be. I believe no one could have supposed that her death would result from the blow. However, you did strike her, and I can't pass it over.

Taking into account the time that Pattison had already served in prison, the judge sentenced him to a further four months in custody. If the Trotter sisters considered this a surprisingly light sentence for such a vicious crime, they could hardly be blamed.

CHAPTER 21

'YOU WOULD SHOOT ONCE TOO OFTEN'

Edmondsley, 1876

John Williams, a thirty-seven-year-old miner, was born in Wales, but he and several members of his family moved to the Durham area to look for work, and he had settled in Edmondsley. Married at the age of nineteen, he and his wife had five children. His widowed mother-in-law Elizabeth Green lived with them, as did Mrs Green's youngest son, Joseph Wales.

On Friday 23 June 1876 John returned from work, had a wash, and went to bed for a short rest. It was pay day, and that evening the joint earnings of himself and his three sons, £6, were brought home by the youngest son and given to Mrs Williams. Between 6 and 7 p.m. John got up and asked his wife where he could find the money. Although she liked a drink or two herself, she was increasingly concerned at the amount he was spending on alcohol, but she knew it would not help her if she did not cooperate. Once he was given the answer, he took a sovereign and went to the Blackhouse Inn, about a mile away. Soon after he had gone, his wife sent their little daughter Mary out to go and fetch him back. Mary soon returned without him, and at length Mrs Williams decided to go and look for him herself. Finding him at the bar, she asked the landlady Margaret Hardy how much money he had brought with him. The landlord James Hardy assured her that her husband had paid everything he owed him.

Mrs Williams then approached her husband. 'What has setten you here?' she asked. 'I see how you are,' he answered. She dug him playfully in the chest, adding, 'You know what that's for.' A man with the temper of John Williams, even when he was sober, was not someone with whom to trifle. He might have tolerated the gesture from his wife in the privacy of their own home but in public, in front of his peers, it was no less than an assault on his dignity. He slapped her in the face, and Mr Hardy asked him to leave. John Williams told him tearfully that he was 'a heartbroken man', and 'would not bide where his wife was'. As he turned to go, the landlord thought he was perfectly sober and just being his usual belligerent self.

Little did anyone know that his temper was about to explode with dangerous consequences. Going home he went into the kitchen and took down his gun, hanging from the rafters. He loaded it with coarse blasting powder from a jug in which he kept a ready supply of powder to be used by himself and his sons in the pits, drove the ramrod in once or twice, and left it in the weapon, protruding slightly from the muzzle. As he walked out of the door with it, his daughter Mary innocently asked him what he was going. He snapped, 'I am going to shoot your mother'.

A worried Mrs Green knew this was no idle threat. She sent for Robert, John Williams' second son, and told him to go and call his father home at once. Putting a shawl over her head she also went out herself in the direction of the Black Horse. She evidently thought that the more people around to try and pacify her aggressive son-in-law the better. On her way she met her two sons, John and Joseph, who had been warned and had the same idea in mind, so she turned back home.

Meanwhile John Williams had been wandering around outside in front of the inn, making no attempt to conceal his gun, and it must have been obvious that here was a tragedy waiting to happen. He returned home without having fired at anybody about forty-five minutes later, between 10 and 11 p.m. When he got home only his small youngest son, another John, daughter Mary and Mrs Green were present. He sat down near the bed with the gun across his knees, and vowed he would shoot the next person to come in. Mrs Green got up and went to the door, warning him angrily, 'you would shoot once too often'. When he told her he did not care, she said she would report him to the police for possessing a gun without a licence. At this he ordered her to get away from the door, or else she 'might catch it'.

She walked to the top of the street where she met John Williams' wife and asked her to fetch the police as he was in an ugly mood. Once she had explained everything, they went back to the house and Mrs Green followed them. Joseph Wales tried the door by lifting the latch, but found it locked from the inside. He asked John Williams to open up, but received no reply. Joseph then put his shoulder to the door so they could get in, followed by his brother John and Mrs Green. The room was well lit by a large fire burning in the grate.

Then John Williams rose from his chair, stepped back, raised the gun to his shoulder, aimed carefully at John Wales from a distance of about three feet, and fired. John Wales fell down at once, his right arm ablaze. The ramrod had entered his shoulder, and went into the lungs, the ferule of the ramrod passing through the upper lobe of the right lung and lodging against the spine. In desperation Mrs Green tried to extinguish the flame from his clothes with her bare hands, and then she found the blood running down. Mrs Williams came in at this point to see what the noise was about, and grabbed the gun from her husband's hands. In her fury she broke it into pieces and threw them into a nearby rain tub.

Dr Linton was called to attend the wounded John Wales. He was in too much agony to be moved from the house, and lingered before dying from his injuries two days later. He was aged twenty-six.

On 5 July Williams was tried at Durham Assizes before Mr Justice Lush, with Mr Edge and Mr Granger appearing for the prosecution, Mr Greenhow for the defence. It must be considered a mark of how much his family hated and feared him that his closest relations were among the main witnesses for the prosecution.

The first to give evidence was Mrs Green. She told the court that sometimes when the prisoner and deceased had been out drinking together in the evening they had their differences, but generally made them up by the next morning. As far as she knew, they had no arguments on the night of the murder. Her son-in-law spent most of his wages on drink, was often drunk at the weekend and sometimes not sober for another day or two. During the week before the killing he had been unusually abstemious, probably as he had attended his mother's funeral a few days earlier. When he arrived with the gun in the evening she thought he was slightly the worse for liquor, but when she saw him loading it, she thought he was preparing a salute for the wedding he had promised to attend a day or two later. It was common knowledge that he needed to keep powder in the house for his work in the pits, and she had never seen him use a gun before.

This evidence was corroborated by Robert Williams, the prisoner's sixteen-year-old second son. He confirmed that his father was drunk nearly every weekend, when he generally spent between 10s and 14s on alcohol. When he had had too much he was not noisy or quarrelsome but more inclined to be 'dull and sulky'.

Joseph Wales, brother of the deceased, said he did not think the prisoner had been drunk that night, an opinion corroborated by the prisoner's fifteen-year-old son John. The eldest son, William, said he had met his father that night coming from the direction of the Black Horse. When he asked his father what he was doing, the answer was 'looking for your mother'. Father, he added, 'was kind of drunky'.

The next witness was Margaret Hardy, who said John Williams came into the taproom at about 7.30 and had something to drink, after which his wife appeared and asked how much money he had brought with him. Though he was asked to go, his wife, who was slightly tipsy, stayed until her brother Joseph arrived, then they went home. When asked to estimate how much the prisoner had drunk at the inn that night, Mrs Hardy said he had only had three pints of ale. She also confirmed that her family had been friends of the Williams family for some years, and that earlier on in the evening he had told her he would bring his gun and have 'a few cracks' at her son's wedding the next day. All the Williams family had been invited as guests.

George Sanor, another miner from Edmondsley, said he went to the Black Horse at around closing up time. He found John Williams standing about thirty yards away, still with the gun in his hands. 'John, let me talk the passion off you,' he said, 'for passion has got the better hold of you.' 'Stand back, George,' was John's answer, 'I'll shoot you as well as any other man.'

Addressing the jury on behalf of the prosecution, Mr Granger said that there was nothing in the evidence to justify reduction of the offence from murder to manslaughter. The prisoner had initially threatened to kill his wife, but ended up deliberately shooting his brother-in-law instead. For the defence, Mr Greenhow said that the prisoner had no motive in killing the deceased, but he must have been drunk as not to be capable of malice or evil intention and that the gun must have gone off by accident.

In summing up, the judge told the jury that there were two questions to be answered. Did the prisoner fire the gun at the deceased, and, if he did, did he know at the time that the gun was charged with ramrod? If the answer to both was yes, then he was guilty of murder. There was nothing to reduce the case to manslaughter. If they were satisfied that the prisoner did not aim the gun at all, but that it went off by accident, he advised them to acquit the prisoner altogether. Under such circumstances, the man would not be guilty of any crime. However, if they concluded that the prisoner did point the weapon at the deceased, but thought it was only loaded with powder, and not also with the ramrod, he would be guilty of manslaughter. If they were satisfied that he knew the gun was loaded with deadly missile and pointed it at the deceased, it was their duty to find him guilty of wilful murder.

The jury took twenty minutes to arrive at the latter conclusion. Donning the black cap, the judge told Williams that nothing in this case could justify him in interfering to save the prisoner from death. If ever there was a case of cold-blooded murder, this was one. It was dreadful to see what drink would do, and the crime was attributed to his drunken habits and the condition in which he was at the time. Although he did not appear very drunk, he knew what he was doing. It also grieved him to find the prisoner's wife also guilty of 'indulging in that dreadful propensity', and it was lamentable that so many offences that came before the Assize Courts were to be attributed to drink. The majority of cases in which it had been his painful duty to pronounce sentence of death had been cases where the criminal had brought himself into that position from self-indulgence. In conclusion, he urged the prisoner not to delude himself with hope that any change would be made in the sentence he was about to pass, but that 'he would look for mercy where it could alone be obtained'. Several petitions were sent to the Secretary of State begging for a reprieve, on the grounds that the killing was unpremeditated and that Williams had been under the influence of alcohol at the time. In view of the testimony that he had initially vowed to shoot his wife and then threatened to kill another, and in view of the assertion of several that he had been at best sober and at worst only slightly the worse for alcohol, they never stood much of a chance. The authorities considered that in view of the recent numerous murders committed in Durham County, an example had to be made.

Some held that a loophole in the licensing laws was partly to blame. A letter from Augustus Granville to *The Times*, published on 10 July, noted that the majority of murders could be traced to drink.

For six days consecutively did this unhappy man procure the means of intoxication at the same public house. Ought this to be possible? The statute provides that no one in liquor shall be supplied with drink, but during the whole of this week preceding the murder as well as on the day of its commission Williams was in a rabid state of intoxication. As a

Inside a Public House, *by John Leech, showing the interior of a typical inn of the mid-nineteenth century*

miserable criminal he is to be hanged, but the landlord who persistently supplied him with the drink goes scot-free, and his licence remains undisturbed as if nothing had happened.

Williams received regular visits from various members of his family, the last on the night of 25 July. As he could not bear thinking of what he had done, he told them, he would be glad when his time had come. At 7 a.m. on 26 July the Revd J. C. Lowe, the prison chaplain, came to see him in his cell. The convicted man appeared sincerely repentant for his crime, and though he blamed members of his family for having been instrumental in bringing him to a death sentence, he freely forgave them. Throughout his imprisonment, he had maintained a stolid indifference as to his impending fate. When he was asked by the prison officers if they could do anything for him, he invariably replied, 'All you can do for me is to get me out of here'.

After a good night's sleep he was roused by the attendant warders at 6 a.m. on 27 July. Williams shed tears for the first time during his imprisonment in a final interview with the chaplain, when he said he forgave his wife, against whom he had previously been so embittered. Just before 8 a.m. he was led to the gallows and executed by Marwood.

CHAPTER 22

DEATH AFTER THE RACES

Tow Law, 1876

Most of the violent deaths in Durham at around this time either resulted from domestic disputes, or else had some Fenian element. One exception to the rule was a case in the summer of 1876 involving two policemen. The *Northern Echo* called it 'one of the most brutal outrages that ever disgraced the county of Durham,' and after the killing of John Hamill, the police had a duty to clear themselves of a strong suspicion by the people of the locality that they had tried to suppress the matter.

The scene of the outrage was known as 'Molly's Open', regarded as one of the wildest and most desolate-looking places in the area. Two miles from Tow Law, on the road between West Auckland and Corbridge, the Travellers' Rest Inn stood on the summit of a hill surrounded by bleak and forbidding moorland. John Howe, the landlord, loosely claimed some men as his neighbours as they lived within a mile or two.

On the night of Monday 29 May 1876, the first day of the Tow Law races, Howe closed at 9.45 p.m., about quarter of an hour early, as there were no customers left. He and the family went to bed, and at about midnight he was awakened by knocking at the door, continuing for fifteen minutes and becoming increasingly violent. He got up, looked out of the window, and saw a tall stout man standing at the front door, demanding to enter.

'You won't get in,' Howe told him.

'Do you know who I am?'

'No, and I don't care.'

'Do you know I'm a policeman?'

'You haven't your uniform, so I won't open the door.'

'I want you to go down with me to fetch another policeman, who is laid down on the road asleep.'

Howe was by now increasingly suspicious of his late and probably intoxicated visitor. 'I won't do anything of the sort.'

The visitor swore and threatened to 'make it worse' for him. He then went round to the window, threw a couple of stones through it, and walked away in the direction of Tow Law. Howe got dressed, went to call on some of his neighbours for help, and began to follow the man. He had only gone about sixty yards from the inn when he heard moaning and saw another man, John Hamill, staggering towards him, blood running from the left side of his head down his chest. It was a light summer night, and he could easily see the full extent of injuries on the man's bare head. He asked him if he had seen another man go down the road with two sticks in his hand.

Hamill said he had and that the man was his attacker. Howe took him back to the Travellers' Rest, and then went in pursuit of the window-breaker whom he realised was probably the same person. On his way he passed four other men, told them what had happened, and they came with him to help. A little further on they caught up with the culprit, Joseph Christison. Howe charged him with breaking the windows and said he would have to go with him. Christison refused and threatened to strike Howe, but the four other men seized him and marched him back to the Travellers' Rest.

Christison had two walking sticks with him, one being a heavy round-headed one. When they were taken from him, this one still had wet blood on it. As he was led into the house, Hamill pointed at him, saying, 'That's the man that's done me, and that's the stick,' pointing to the thick one as he added, 'I wouldn't have cared if he hadn't come a second time at me.'

Howe then went out and yoked his pony, to ride to Tow Law for a policeman. One of his friends, George Hardy, a quarryman from Greenfield Cottages, about a hundred yards from the Travellers' Rest, went to Tow Law with the trap, and Howe returned to the house. At about 1 a.m. another drunken man came to the door, and demanded to be let in. 'Smash in, Watson,' Christison called out to him, 'the bastards are filling drink all ends up.'

Henry Watson, who was evidently Christison's friend, tried to force his way in but failed, so he went round to the back and smashed thirteen window panes, leaving only three intact. He then started breaking the frames, and Howe asked some of the others inside to go and bring him in before he did any more damage. Once they had done so, both the drunks were detained until Hardy brought Police Constable John Edwards along, and they were given into custody.

When Edwards arrived, Watson said that he was a policeman and Edwards could not arrest him. He gave his name, number and address, but Christison refused to follow likewise. Howe told Edwards it was his duty to take the men into custody, whoever they might be. The two prisoners actively resisted and had to be taken to Tow Law by force. Howe took the stick from Christison, but as they were nearing Tow Law, Christison grabbed it from his hand, saying it belonged to him. Howe then told Edwards what he had been using it for. At about 2.30 a.m. the men were given into the charge of Police Sergeant George Coverdale, on a charge of breaking windows. Nothing was said at this time about the assault on Hamill. Coverdale proceeded to search the taller of the two men, and while doing so he said, 'You will not lock me up, sergeant; you know well enough who it was.'

To his astonishment, Coverdale found he was dealing with as a fellow policeman. 'Christison, is that you?' he asked. 'What have you been getting into this scrape for?'

'Sergeant, we have done nothing,' was the answer; 'those men waylaid us, and you can see we have got the worst of it.'

Coverdale then recognised the other man as Constable Henry Watson, whom he knew to be stationed at Blackhill. Unaware of the assault on Hamill, he let them go in return for a promise not to interfere with Howe's house again. They were warned that he would have to report the charge of wilful damage against them to Superintendent Oliver at Consett, but he had no power to detain them for such a trivial offence.

Howe and his companions then returned wearily to the Travellers' Rest. It was not yet the end of a long, disturbed night, for at 4 a.m. the prisoners returned to the inn and tried to force an entrance. Mrs Howe, heavily pregnant at the time, had been keeping watch out of the back window. Both men were in an even more belligerent mood by now and threatened to 'knock their brains out' when they got inside the inn. After what had already happened, Howe was taking no chances and he continued to guard the broken back window. Christison still had his stick with him, but as he and Watson could not get in, they gave up and walked back towards Castleside.

Meanwhile, on Edwards's advice, the injured Hamill was taken back to Tow Law. Next day he was taken to Revd Mr De Pledge, JP, who advised him to go and see Superintendent Oliver at Consett. He went there but did not find Mr Oliver, so Howe took him back to his home at Dean House and left him in the care of his landlord.

The two policemen would probably have escaped with little more than a severe reprimand, had it not been for the fact that Hamill's injuries proved far more severe than they had seemed at first. He died at 9 a.m. on Thursday 1 June, less than three days after the attack, and the charge became one of suspected murder.

An inquest was held by the coroner, Mr Graham, at the Travellers' Rest on 3 June. Neither Christison nor anyone else was present on his behalf. Among those who attended were Sergeant Coverdale, Constable Edwards, Superintendent James Oliver from Consett and Superintendent Thubrow from Wolsingham. After going to Prospect Place to view the body, the jury returned to the inn to hear the coroner's evidence.

Howe was the first to speak as he recounted the events of Monday night. He was followed by Aaron Hurst, a quarryman from Prospect Place, where Hamill had lodged with him, who confirmed that he had seen the thirty-nine-year-old injured man die on Thursday morning.

Another quarryman, Isaac Ebdon, from Molly's Open, had been called by Howe on Monday at about midnight, and on going down the road had seen Howe and Hamill together, the latter with blood running down his face. They took him back to the Rest, washed his head, and found two wounds on the left side of his forehead, so large that they could have put a finger inside. There was another cut on the crown of his head, although not bleeding as badly as the others. He put some sticking plaster on, but it failed to stop the blood from coming through. Shortly after that Howe appeared, leading another man, whereupon Hamill pointed at the latter, declaring that was the man who had knocked him down. The man told Hamill that he was not going to be detained by anyone.

'There is plenty to detain you for,' Hamill told him. 'You have knocked this man [himself] down, broken Howe's windows, and you will not get out here until the police come, no matter how long that may be.' When the man denied it was him, Howe turned to Hamill and asked if he was sure this man was the culprit. Hamill said he would swear that it was. Two further witnesses, Adam Holmes, a farm labourer from Low Hermitage, and George Ayre, from Springwell Cottage, both confirmed Howe's version of events.

The first policeman to speak was Edwards, who said that after receiving information at 1 a.m. on Tuesday morning, he accompanied Hardy to the Travellers' Rest. When he arrived, Howe gave the two men into custody, both for wilful damage by breaking his window, and one for also assaulting Hamill. One of them, the one charged only with damage, gave a false name and number, while his companion refused to give his name and address but said he was a policeman. Both prisoners put up a mild show of resistance at first before being taken away. Despite his injuries Hamill walked with them to Tow Law, and it was noticed that he still seemed as talkative and lively as any of the others.

At this point, a juryman commented that he thought it advisable to exclude Coverdale, the other policeman involved, from the room where Edwards was giving his evidence. The coroner said that Coverdale's evidence did not bear upon that given by Edwards. He might say that, instead of trying to screen the police, the superintendents present appeared to have done their best to get all the evidence they reasonably could, and there seemed to be no suspicion that they were perverting the course of justice by trying to protect their own. The juror answered that there had been some talk about Coverdale 'liberating' the men, but the coroner observed that in doing so, the sergeant had acted perfectly within his jurisdiction. He could not even detain them if they had been charged with assault.

Resuming, Coverdale said that the prisoners had left Tow Law Police Station immediately. He had promised he would go back to Howe's house later that morning, and only when he did so was he told fully about the attack. On the road he met Superintendent Oliver and gave him all the information he had obtained about the alleged assault and damage. At that time he had no idea how serious the assault was, let alone of the likely consequences. The latter only became apparent on Wednesday, when he took Dr George Johnston of Tow Law to Hamill's lodgings, and found his condition had deteriorated. He then reported the matter to Oliver, in whose custody Christison was by then.

Oliver said he had apprehended Christison on Friday 2 June and charged him with causing the death of Hamill. Christison made no reply, and Oliver then searched his house for the stick with which he had attacked him, but failed to find it.

Dr Johnston testified to having first seen Hamill between midday and 1 p.m. on Wednesday, examined him in bed, looked at the wounds and the blackened left eye. He tried to ask Hamill questions but found him unable to speak, though conscious of pain when he pricked him and probably suffering from concussion or compression of the brain. He visited him again between 9 and 10 p.m. in the evening, and found no change in his condition. Coverdale was also present, and Johnston gave him a certificate stating that the man's life was in danger. He was sent for a third time on Thursday morning, but before he could arrive Hamill was dead. In conjunction with Dr Hood he made a post-mortem examination on Thursday 2 June. They found that the cause of death was a fractured skull, or effusion of blood on the brain as a result of violence. It was unlikely that the injury had been self-inflicted, and the victim must have been subjected to considerable violence. A blow from a heavy, round-headed stick, or from any blunt instrument applied with sufficient force, would have been enough.

After the coroner had summed up, the jury retired for half an hour. They found Christison guilty of wilful murder, but without premeditation. When the coroner remarked upon the verdict, the foreman said that the jury believed Christison did not intend to kill the man. Another juror said that if the coroner and others would again retire, the jury would consider the matter again. Another few minutes' deliberation followed, then they produced an amended verdict to the effect that Christison had caused Hamill's death, 'and we find him guilty of wilful murder'.

Further proceedings followed at Lanchester Petty Sessions on 8 June, with Henry Marshall giving evidence for the prosecution, and John Patrick for the defence. When Constable Edwards was questioned further, he was asked why he had not told Sergeant Coverdale about the assault on Hamill as well as the wilful damage at the inn. Edwards said he thought Hamill only had a slight cut, and did not think it was serious. He was not bleeding as badly as Watson. Sergeant Coverdale said they could not hold the prisoners at Tow Law as they had no charge-room there, and though they were discharged, they were warned they would be hearing more about their misdemeanours that night. Hamill had said nothing to the police that night about any intention to lay a charge of assault against the prisoner, and at the time he was 'in a competent state to do so if he wished'. It was clear that everyone involved, including Hamill himself, had underestimated the severity of his injuries at the time.

George Johnston was next to give evidence, backed by Dr George Hood of Tow Law, who was also present at the post-mortem. He said that if Hamill travelled seventeen miles on the Tuesday in a gig, it would certainly aggravate any symptoms or the effect of injuries. The court suggested that if he had been put to bed, kept quiet and his wounds attended to at once, he might have had a better chance of survival. There was no displacement of the frontal bone, and it was merely a simple fracture. Riding in a gig would tend to increase the effusion of blood on the brain, and therefore the danger, as the outcome of events had proved.

Police Sergeant William Masterman of Consett said that on the morning of 30 May Hamill had come to the police station with Howe. He asked to see Superintendent Oliver, who was away. At the time he had a cut on his head, which had been plastered up. Christison's solicitor then made an objection to any statement made by Hamill to Masterman being given in court. Oliver said that on 2 June he took the prisoner into custody, charged with causing the death of Hamill.

When asked for his explanation of events, Watson said he and Christison were both constables in Oliver's division. They been drinking heavily on the racecourse at Tow Law and left together at about 6 p.m. on Monday. He could recall nothing of what took place on the road from Tow Law during the next few hours.

At this point information was received by the court that Watson's case had been disposed of by Mr Clavering in the second court, that of Christison having been heard in the first, and that he had only ordered Watson to pay damages. Somebody else said that Watson had tried to reach a compromise with Howe by paying for the damage he had caused at the Travellers' Rest, including expenses. At once there was speculation that the police authorities had tried to hush the matter up as far as Watson was involved. The magistrates objected and ordered his case to be taken after that of Christison was settled. Mr Depledge said that Howe told him Watson's case had been carried into the other court, and if he did not appear the case would be struck out. Howe stepped forward, and in answer to the chairman, Mr Kearney, said that when he went into the second court he told Mr Clavering that magistrates in that court wished to hear the case.

Kearney said that there appeared to have been a miscarriage of justice. Mr Kidson said that for a policeman to break into a man's house and to be allowed to compromise the offence 'was really too bad for anything' and a reflection upon all concerned. 'Here is a policeman who coolly breaks into a man's house at night, and that he should be allowed to compromise this offence is too bad for anything. He ought to have been brought up here and punished.' The normal punishment for such a misdemeanour was £5 or two months' imprisonment. Watson, he thought, deserved the severest punishment that could be handed down for his conduct. The chairman remarked that they had better say no more about it. Watson was dismissed from the police force in disgrace, and the magistrates duly committed Christison for trial for wilful murder at the next Durham Assizes.

The case was heard before Mr Justice Lush on Tuesday 4 July, with Mr Campbell Foster QC and Mr Sowerby for the prosecution, and Mr Maule, QC, and Mr Edge for the defence.

Among those giving evidence for the prosecution were John and Jane Howe, Isaac Hebden, Adam Holmes, Thomas Milburn, James Cowling, George Ayre and Hannah Stirk. Dr George Johnson was there again to describe the injuries sustained by John Hamill. Three local clergymen, as well as Superintendent Wood of Gateshead Police and various others gave character references on behalf of the prisoner.

In his summing up, Mr Foster said that if Christison willfully struck Hamill and caused death, it was murder. It would be the duty of Mr Maule to offer an excuse on behalf of the prisoner, and he would be happy if he could reduce the crime to one of manslaughter. If there was no excuse for the prisoner and nothing to reduce the crime then it would be the jury's duty to find the prisoner guilty of murder.

On the prisoner's behalf, Mr Maule commented on the excellent character reference he had been given. He said that the prosecution had set up what would be an improbable story against any man, but how much more improbable was it when told of a man like the prisoner, who was the least likely to be implicated in it. The prisoner had acted from the best of intentions in trying to get aid for his helplessly drunk companion Watson, and this was the only reason he had gone to Howe's house. There was no witness as to what took place when Hamill was injured; what actually happened would never be known, and it was not for the prosecution to come up with 'suggestions and fancies' of their own. Hamill might have been drunk and assaulted Christison. If they were guided by the strict law of evidence, they would either say that the offence amounted only to manslaughter, or that it was accidental and unintended by the prisoner.

The jury retired for twenty-five minutes, and returned a verdict of manslaughter, the foreman declaring that it had not been intentional.

The judge told Christison he had had a very narrow escape, and hoped it would be a warning not only to him but to all others 'against indulging in that dreadful vice which transforms men into brutes'. It had been 'a reckless, wicked act', and Christison was sentenced to penal servitude for twenty years.

CHAPTER 23

'I ALWAYS THOUGHT I WOULD BE HANGED'

Sunderland, 1878

26 June 1878 was an exceptionally hot day in Sunderland, with temperatures well into the nineties. One of the ships waiting for the wind to pick up in order to set sail was the *William Leckie*, where a twenty-strong crew sat under blazing sun ready to sail for Buenos Aires. The captain, Lumley Fletcher, was well known as a firm disciplinarian, and the pilot, John Wallace, was a well-respected seaman.

After returning on board at about 4.30 that afternoon from a business meeting, the captain was not happy with what he found. The new cook, Robert Vest, a stocky man with a badly scarred weather-beaten face and a broken nose, who had been engaged to feed the crew, was sitting around, waving his arms and mumbling incoherently as other members of the crew sat around playing violins. The captain told Vest that such behaviour would not be tolerated. He must leave the cabin and go into the deckhouse, and he would 'put him square' in the morning. (According to another account, Fletcher ordered Vest to pack up his belongings, and go ashore immediately, as he refused to carry a drunken man on board.) As the captain finished speaking, he tried to say something but Wallace, standing by smoking his pipe, interrupted in a jocular manner, 'come aft, boys, and out him in irons'. While the captain and pilot returned to their cabins, Vest stumbled to the galley and sobbed.

The rations of grog were given out as usual later that afternoon, but none was given to Vest, except for a teaspoonful by one of the apprentices who took pity on him and gave him some from his own portion.

By the evening Vest was sitting quietly on the deck. While the captain and chief mate were having tea in the cabin, he saw Wallace go past his door. He went and grabbed a ten-inch knife, ran and grabbed hold of Wallace, who had been in the water-closet, slashed his throat and then plunged the knife up his bowels. Wallace fell to the floor, screaming, 'Boys, I'm stabbed!' He lay choking as he tried to pull the knife from his body, while the captain shouted for bandages and brandy, to stop the loss of blood.

Within seconds Wallace's life had ebbed away, and his body was covered with the ship's flag as a mark of respect. Vest offered no resistance as he was tied to the deck while the captain ran a distress signal for help to come from ashore. Over an hour later Inspector James Larkin of the River Police Station in Low Street and other officers reached the ship. By now Vest was starting to ramble. Tom Talbot, an apprentice who was guarding him, later said he was sure Vest was drunk at the time. He had heard Wallace crying out that he was stabbed, and found him standing with one foot in the water closet and the other out. Vest was standing beside him, and had hold of him with his right hand, holding his collar with the other. Wallace's trousers were down, and Talbot saw a large knife in the prisoner's right hand.

Talbot struck his arm and tried to stop the blow, when he saw Vest was about to stab his victim a second time. Talbot turned round to get a belaying pin. Looking round, he saw Vest take the knife, draw it back, plunge it into Wallace's bowels and leave it there, all but about two inches of the knife being hidden. Wallace fell forward and died immediately.

Vest then pulled the knife out and threw it on the deck. As he was being lashed to the deck, he said to Talbot, 'I hope that the poor man is gone, and that his soul has gone to heaven.' He also said that for about twenty years he had been having bad dreams of hangings and murders, and always thought that one day he would be hanged. He also said, 'Tommy, you see the effects of drink.' Before they left the ship, Vest said, 'It's all right, I plead guilty; I have done it.' Later he said, 'There's something at the bottom of this; you know the pilot and the captain are to blame for this. I won't say anything about it now.'

After being taken to the steam tug, and while being removed to the police station, he said to the constable, 'I saw Wallace in the water-closet; he looked at me and I looked at him, and I looked at the knife in the galley. I walked along the deck a bit. Something said to me, "go out and finish him". I deliberately went and drew the knife out of the galley and did the deed. I am sorry I did not see the captain; he would have shared the same fate.'

The police sergeant told him it was a pity he had done it. Vest then said, 'I am only sorry for my wife and five daughters. For the last twenty years, I have read all kinds of books about all kinds of murders, and I always thought I would be hanged.'

When Wallace's body was examined, a cut was found across the throat, his finger and thumb were slashed as if he had seized the knife in an effort to protect himself, and his bowels were protruding from a terrible gash in his stomach. Two days later the jury went to the victim's home at 13 Peel Street to view the body. An inquest was held around the corner in the home of Hugh McAllister, Salem House, Salem Street, Hendon.

On 8 July, four days before the trial, a correspondent from the *Northern Echo* published some interesting details about the prisoner and his past. Since being confined in Durham Gaol he had retained 'a dogged, sullen demeanour', and the officials were keeping a strict watch over him at all times. The slightest avoidable interruption produced what might be termed excessive passion, which he had shown ever since he first became known in Seaham Harbour, where more than half a dozen times he had been seen brandishing knives in a threatening attitude, causing intense alarm to everybody else around. About a week after being released from Durham Gaol on a charge of violently assaulting Mr

Sunderland, looking east along the Wear River, late nineteenth century © Paul Head

White, the Seaham gas manager, he was walking in the company of a Seaham Harbour resident from Sunderland to the former place, when his language about murdering by shooting or stabbing was so alarming that before they had gone two miles, his companion returned to Sunderland on the pretence that he had forgotten something.

Moreover he had once tried to walk on a rope a distance of ten yards to board a vessel lying in Seaham Docks, in order to carry out a threat made to a seaman against whom he had a long-standing grudge, when he fell into the water. Another time he walked out of a good job for the reason that he discovered his employers were realising 6 per cent profit, insisting he would sooner break stones upon a highway for 2s per day than work for those who made fortunes out of exploiting the working classes. He gave up another post as he had decided he would write the history of his life, having persuaded himself or been persuaded that it would sell in thousands at 2s 6d per copy, and he would be able to retire for life on the proceeds. When people laughed at him, he lost his temper, tore up the manuscript and burnt it.

'When a soldier,' he was quoted as saying, 'I in duty to my country killed and slayed many innocent beings who never did me the slightest injury; then why cannot I kill my enemies, which I will do, and will be hanged for it.' Had the captain made full enquiries as to Vest's history, it was unlikely he would have engaged him.

Ships on River Wear, Sunderland, late nineteenth century

On 12 July the trial of Vest opened at Durham Assizes. Mr John Edge and Mr Hans Hamilton prosecuted, and Mr Blackwell defended. Captain Lumley Fletcher was the first witness called for the prosecution. He said that when he went on board at about 4 p.m., he noticed Vest was drunk, and asked him what he meant by being in such a state when he held such a responsible position. He told him he would not have a man on board in the state he was in, would not tolerate such conduct, and intended to send him ashore. A little later he relented, and was prepared to give Vest another chance, saying, 'Stop you there until tomorrow morning and I will put you square, and make you duty as an ordinary seaman.'

Mr Blackwell said that had it not been for the clergyman, the prisoner would probably not have been defended at all. Mr Haswell, who had undertaken Vest's defence at the preliminary trial, had been unable to obtain any witnesses until the last moment, as the prisoner had only been committed for trial during the previous week. Until the last two or three days, nothing had been done. During the morning four or five had been collected, but he had had no chance to consult with them yet, and he had no idea what they would reveal about the previous history of the prisoner. He asked the judge to give him a little time to confer with them, and would then be in a position to say whether he needed to call any more witnesses or not. The judge consented, allowing them thirty minutes.

When they reassembled, Blackwell called the witnesses. Vest's brother Thomas, an engine fitter from Spennymoor, said that when he was sixteen Robert enlisted in the 16th Regiment of Foot, and was sent to India. While he was there he went into the Horse Artillery instead and served during the Crimean War. He was discharged because of wounds sustained in battle and was sent home. When Thomas saw him, he had a wound on his temple, and told Thomas it was a bayonet wound he had received during an engagement. He also mentioned several times that he had been affected by sunstroke in India, one of the reasons why he had joined the Horse Artillery.

The charge of the light brigade in the Crimean War, in which Robert Vest served

Before joining the army he had had a tendency to walk for miles in his sleep. His companions often had to wake him up when he reached the gas works where he was employed, as he sometimes walked several miles too far.

In 1877 Thomas visited Robert, who said he had been at Bilbao, was very depressed and sometimes thought about committing suicide. Ann Graham, their sister, of Chester-le-Street, said Robert had often visited her at her home. After he entered on the seafaring life, she saw cuts on his forehead, which he explained had been caused by falling between two ships. Though he sometimes seemed capable of violence towards others, he was always kindly and well-behaved to his wife and children.

On behalf of the prisoner, Mr Blackwell said that not a single word was uttered before the deed was committed to show that Vest had any ill feeling towards Wallace. He asked the jury to consider the whole of the circumstances surrounding the case, and urged that the mental condition of the prisoner at the time did not enable him to control his actions. The only evidence against him was that he was drunk. On that swelteringly hot day in June, he had been driven by an irresistible impulse which came upon him. The first time Wallace went into the water-closet was the first time he had any idea of committing the deed, and it was committed by him during a state of temporary insanity, when his judgment between right and wrong was impaired.

His wife and five daughters, who lived in Seaham, watched him from the courtroom as he pleaded 'not guilty' to murder. It was reported at the time that Vest had five terrible scars on his forehead and a large dent on the side of his head, but when asked he could

Sunderland Quayside © Paul Head

not explain how he had got his scars, only saying that they caused him terrible pain. It was strongly argued by the defence that Vest must have committed the act while in a state of temporary insanity.

His relatives were able to supply further details. At the age of seventeen he had joined the army, the 16th Regiment of Infantry, then transferred to the Horse Artillery, and while serving in India he suffered from sunstroke. Later he was a gunner in the Crimean War between 1854 and 1856, during which thousands of British soldiers lost their lives through strategic errors by their commanding officers, while many more died from disease or starvation. The War Office sent a letter to the court telling how Vest had suffered head injuries when an artillery shell had exploded close to him. His family also explained that during a Russian attack he had been wounded in the forehead with a bayonet or a saber and had been badly scarred ever since. Before going to fight in the war, his brother said, he was 'a very steady young man', but after returning home from the Crimea he had often suffered from severe pain and depression.

At this point a surgeon, Dr Matthew Francis, was called in to see what level his sanity had been affected by the injuries. If they had been inflicted twenty years or more previously, they would be enough to cause loss of sanity in such hot conditions. The prosecution disagreed, maintaining that he must have committed the offence while under the influence of alcohol, although no witnesses had seen Vest drinking that day.

In summing up, the judge said that Blackwell had been wise to put forward a plea of temporary insanity, as no other excuse could reasonably have been argued. The jury, he said, must be satisfied that the prisoner was labouring from the effects of a diseased mind

Sunderland High Street

to such an extent as to cause him not to know the character or the nature of the deed he was committing, before they returned a verdict of acquittal on the grounds of insanity. Or to put it another way, did they think the prisoner would have committed such an act if a policeman had been standing nearby at the time? If they believed that Vest killed the man without being under any such influence and in a sane state of mind then they would surely have no hesitation in finding him guilty of wilful murder.

The jury retired at 4.15 p.m. and returned at 5.40 with a verdict of 'guilty' but with a strong recommendation to mercy, hoping he would be sent to Broadmoor Criminal Lunatic Asylum. However, Mr Justice Baggalley donned the black cap to say that the law imposed on him 'the duty of passing sentence of death upon every person convicted before me of the crime of wilful murder. I have no discretion in the matter.'

Names were collected from people in Sunderland, Durham, Chester-le-Street and Seaham for a petition, as well as for money for his wife and family. Dr Smith of Sedgefield and the Revd Blunt of Chester-le-Street led a joint campaign for a detailed enquiry into Vest's mental condition, but without success.

On the morning of 30 July 1878, Vest's eyes were red and swollen after an uneasy night. As the hangman went to pinion his arms and legs, he begged him to wait until he had shaken hands with everybody present, then turned to the chaplain as the hood and noose were placed over his head, saying that he would pray for them in Heaven. As he reached the scaffold he prayed fervently, and was heard to say several times, 'Lord Jesus, receive my soul'. Of all the convicted killers executed in Durham during the decade, in view of his history and subsequent mental condition there can be little doubt that he was the one least responsible for the actions which led him to the scaffold.

CHAPTER 24

THE FIGHT AT THE COLLIERY INN

South Wingate, 1878

On the evening of 2 March 1878 twenty-eight-year-old James Doyle, a labourer employed on the new railway line being built between Sunderland and Stockton, went to Hartbushes with a fellow labourer, Luke Moore. After buying some provisions they went to the Colliery Inn, South Wingate, kept by Emmanuel Young, where Doyle quarrelled with another patron, though no blows were struck. Doyle and Moore then went into the bar, where they stood around drinking for nearly an hour. At about 9.30 William Bagnall (or William Gallon, according to some reports), a miner living at South Wingate, came into the bar, accused Doyle of having hit him on a previous occasion and hit him in the face with the back of his open hand. Doyle collapsed in the passage, unconscious. Young picked him up and took him into the backyard.

Nothing more was done until closing time at 11 p.m. when Doyle was still lying in the yard. Moore and Young both tried to speak to him, but he did not answer, so they went away and left him lying there. Constable Hawkins, who was doing a routine check on the premises and was unaware of any incidents earlier on, asked Young for a wheelbarrow to take the prostrate man away, but the landlord did not have one. Nobody thought to call a doctor, as presumably nobody thought he had been seriously injured. Young put him in the stable overnight and went to bed.

Next morning, at about 5.30, Mrs Young went into the stable and found Doyle still lying there insensible. Increasingly concerned that he was actually ill, they took him into the bar, and placed him in front of the fire. He rallied slightly, so the landlord gave him some brandy and then tea, which he swallowed with some difficulty.

Thinking all he needed was peace and quiet, Young took him back into the stable and placed him on a bed of straw, where he lay until midday on Sunday. Hawkins came back to check, with the intention of charging him with being drunk. When he was rather belatedly told about the incident on the previous evening, he ordered a horse and cart. Still unconscious, Doyle was still insensible, and taken to Mr Thompson's, where he lodged at Hurworth Burn, about two miles from the Colliery Inn. Dr Wilson of Castle Eden was sent for, arrived about 12.00 on Monday, examined Doyle and said there was nothing that could be done for him. An hour later he was dead.

Bagnall, a married man with two children, was apprehended and charged with being responsible for his death. An inquest was opened by Mr Maynard on 7 March and adjourned until the next day. When Bagnall was charged at Castle Eden Police Court, Young was the only witness to offer evidence. When the chairman of the magistrates asked if he had given Doyle anything before going to bed on Saturday night, the landlord said he had not. 'I did not know what the matter was with him, as I did not think he was drunk.' 'It seems very inhuman,' was the chairman's response.

Bagnall was committed to the next Durham Assizes on a charge of manslaughter. On his behalf Mr Bentham applied for bail, but it was refused as the bench said it was a very serious case. He was tried on 22 March, found guilty of manslaughter, and sentenced to one month with hard labour.

CHAPTER 25

THE EXCITED MRS PRINSKY

West Hartlepool, 1879

On 22 October 1879 the magistrates at West Hartlepool investigated a case of domestic violence, brought at the instance of Superintendent Marley, acting on information given him by neighbours. In the dock was Moses Prinsky, a Jew by birth, who ran a jewellery and tobacconist business in Albert Street, West Hartlepool. He was charged with having assaulted his mentally deranged wife Blumah and subjecting her to systematic ill treatment. Mrs Prinsky, who was looking rather haggard, was present by order of the court and confined to a chair, where she remained throughout the hearing.

Mr E. Harrison appeared for the prosecution and Mr E. Bell for the defence. Charles Foreman, who lived next door, was the first to be called as a witness. He said that at 8.30 on the morning of 17 October he heard a woman crying out loud, went and looked over the wall to see what was going on, and saw the defendant thrashing his wife in one of the upper rooms. He was beating her for nearly quarter of an hour, and she screamed so loudly that she was attracting the attention of people in the street. He struck her on her head.

When cross-examined by Mr Bell, he said that the Prinskys' eighteen-year-old son was present. Foreman told Prinsky that he thoroughly deserved to be beaten in the same manner, but the latter replied that she deserved it because she was killing his son. Gilbert Dyer stated that he also mounted the wall and saw the defendant holding his wife firmly by the arm or wrist, apparently in the act of striking her.

Charles Braithwaite, a youth who lived in the same street, said that some three weeks previously, he had seen Mrs Prinsky in the yard, 'in an excited state', heard her shouting, and apparently having some difficulty in breathing. Prinsky was leaning over her, and Braithwaite thought perhaps she had been shut out of doors. Mr Boanson said that he had often heard screams during the past three years, and about three weeks previously, as mentioned by the previous witness, Mrs Prinsky was shut outside the house. He thought she had suffered from want of proper food and nourishment, and when he warned the defendant about it his only answer was that his wife would not eat properly.

George Chambers, who kept a pork butcher's shop next door to the defendant, said that disturbances had taken place there on a regular basis during the previous four years. Three

Hartlepool, c.1865 (© Paul Head)

weeks earlier Mrs Prinsky had been shut out of the house, and on Friday 17 October he heard her screaming. He had often been awakened in the middle of the night by noise, and all he could do was knock on the wall and hope they would be quiet. Alfred Blackburn had seen the defendant pulling his wife upstairs by the hair of her head and her arms.

Dr Gourley said that he saw the woman on Friday evening. She was by herself in a little back kitchen, and there was not the slightest sign of comfort or attention and no food. When he spoke to her she complained bitterly of her husband's ill treatment, he standing by meantime, but she declined to be examined and became excited. He had no doubt her mind was affected, and the treatment to which she was said to have been subjected would be sufficient to account for her derangement.

In reply to the bench, Dr Gourley added that he did not think Mrs Prinsky was sufficiently sound to give evidence. She was tolerably coherent when he saw her on Friday, but she soon became excited. In his opinion, she had not received proper supervision.

Before proceeding with the defence the bench, on their own account, required the independent testimony of Mrs Prinsky's brother, Mr Isaac Kaufman, tobacconist, of Hartlepool. He had not seen his sister for about eighteen months, but he knew that her husband was in the habit of beating her. On one occasion he hit her eight or nine times, and Isaac had to intervene. Finding that his sister was being shamefully neglected, he had her removed to Lady Montefiore's institution, and afterwards to Croydon.

For the defence the son, Solomon Prinsky, was called, and he denied that his father ever struck his mother or deprived her of food. As to the business on Friday morning, he said that his mother, in a fit of violence, jumped on to a box and smashed several articles, and he tried to calm her down. All this alleged ill treatment, he said, was necessary restraint. On the morning in question, she had also broken a window and then grabbed him by his shirt, and he found it necessary to call his father for help.

One of the daughters, Isabella Prinsky, gave evidence which corroborated that of her brother. In answer to the bench, she stated that her mother never sat down with the rest of the family to meals. Dr Mackenzie, her regular medical attendant, stated that since the birth of a child three years before, Mrs Prinsky had been 'in a low state' and 'more or less insane'. While she complained of violence inflicted on her by the husband, she refused to let the doctor examine her, even though for him to have done so would have proved her allegations. He was informed that sometimes she had not taken any food for days. After having several conversations with her, he thought it would be best if she was kept in a place of confinement, where she would be properly treated and cared for.

The magistrates retired for consultation, and on their return they announced that they considered the case proved beyond all doubt. They were satisfied that the defendant had cruelly ill-treated his wife and neglected her. For the assault Prinsky was fined £5, or two months' imprisonment, and for the good of the family as well as her own, Mrs Prinsky would be sent to an asylum.

CHAPTER 26

MISCELLANY

Manslaughter, Barnard Castle, 1870

A family argument in February 1870 ended in death. John Kellett, aged fifty-one, who lived at Woodland, near Barnard Castle, had an altercation with his son-in-law Thomas Bambridge, aged twenty-one, at about midnight, which ended in the younger man being shot dead. An inquest was held on 16 February at Woodland before Mr T. Dean, deputy coroner for Darlington. It was established that Bambridge was married to Kellett's daughter, and for the previous three months she had been living with her father because she was unwell.

On the night of Saturday 12 February, Bambridge went to see his wife at Kellett's house. Finding the door locked, he tried to gain entry by force. Kellett was ready for him and had taken down his double-barrelled gun. A struggle ensued, and both parties decided to settle the matter outside. Kellett pointed the gun at his son-in-law and fired, the contents lodging in his left side, and he died the following afternoon.

During the morning Kellett had been apprehended and taken into custody, charged with unlawful wounding, and the inquest jury returned a verdict of wilful murder. He appeared at Durham Assizes before Mr Justice Willes on 1 March, was found guilty of the lesser charge of manslaughter and was sentenced to ten years' penal servitude.

Assault, Shincliffe, 1870

George Howard and Mr Wood were coke drawers who lived and worked together at Shincliffe. Mr Howard was inclined to be argumentative, if not actually violent, by nature. On 21 November he became involved in a dispute with Mr Wood and the latter's wife. When matters threatened to get out of hand, she tried to stop him from physically attacking her husband. He went for her with a knife, leaving her badly wounded.

Howard appeared before Durham County Magistrates' Court on 3 December, charged with assault. A witness for the prosecution, the surgeon Mr W. C. Blackett, who had been

Shincliffe Village

*The discovery of the body of Isabella Young (*Illustrated Police News*)*

looking after Mrs Wood, gave evidence as to the extent of her injuries. He said it was unlikely that she would ever make a full recovery. The prisoner was sentenced to four months' hard labour and an additional two months for non-payment of costs.

MURDER AND SUICIDE, BLACKHILL, 1872

For some time, it was said, Isabella Young, the wife of a papermaker who lived at Blackhill, had been 'in a morbid state of mind through suffering'. Early on the afternoon of 27 May she took two of her children to a secluded spot, Bridge Hill. Leaving the baby in a perambulator beside the road, she took the elder child into the wood and tried to cut her throat. The girl broke free from her and ran home, her clothes covered in blood. Mrs

Young then took the baby, stabbed her in the stomach, and then cut her own throat from ear to ear. Two men walking past heard the baby's screams, and by the time they reached the scene, Mrs Young was dead. The baby had her arm around her mother's neck. At first it was feared that she would die as well, but her wounds were not life-threatening, and like her sister she went on to make a full recovery.

At the inquest at Blackhill on 5 June, the verdict on Mrs Young was that she had cut her throat 'while in an unsound state of mind'.

DEAD DRUNK, SUNDERLAND BRIDGE, 1873

At about 4 a.m. on 22 December 1873, a gang of men employed at the coke ovens at Bronney Colliery saw a man lying beside the road. They tried to arouse him, but without success. When they got hold of a light and shone it on him, they found he was bleeding heavily from several wounds on the head. There was deep cut above his left eye, and also a cut in the hat corresponding with the same. He died a few minutes after being found.

It was later found that he was sixty-year-old Thomas Farthing, employed as a platelayer at Messrs Bell Brothers collieries. He was known to have been drinking at an Irish public house in Sunderland Bridge for much of Sunday, and boasting that he had a considerable sum of money on him. At about 7 p.m. he went to the Three Horse Shoes Inn, but was so drunk that the landlord refused to serve him. He stayed about half an hour and then staggered out.

His body was found about 250 yards away from the inn. Nearby was a purse containing ten sovereigns, and some silver scattered around. A navvy who had been seen in his company on Sunday was taken into custody by the police, to await the inquest on 23 December.

When the inquest took place before the deputy coroner, Mr Dean, nothing was found to link the navvy with Farthing's death, and he was released. The jury returned the following verdict:

That the deceased came by his death from a fall whilst drunk and incapable; that the publican who supplied him with the drink is responsible for his death. We are also of opinion that the licensing magistrates are morally responsible for the excessive drunkenness and crimes of frightful violence which prevail in this district.

MANSLAUGHTER, SHADFORTH, 1874

At Durham Spring Assizes at the Crown Court on 4 March 1874, before Mr Justice Denman, twenty-two-year-old John Black was charged with the manslaughter of George Lonsdale at Shadforth on 1 November 1873. Mr Greenhow prosecuted, and Mr Wright defended. For the prosecution, Mr Greenhow said that on the day in question Lonsdale, aged about seventy, a publican at Thornley, was sitting in his bar when the prisoner went into the house extremely inebriated and demanded yet more to drink. Lonsdale told him he had had more than enough already, and ordered him to leave the premises. Black went out but returned soon afterwards and insisted on being served. Lonsdale tried to push him out, and a struggle ensued in which he was pushed down on to a fender and badly injured. A doctor was called, examined him and found that he had sustained a severe head wound, and 'depression of the bone'.

Lonsdale never recovered and died on 30 November. The learned counsel pointed out that if they, the jury, were satisfied that the prisoner was unlawfully resisting his ejection, any injury he inflicted in the scuffle that resulted in the publican's death, even though there might be no evil intent, would still render him guilty of manslaughter. After a lengthy absence, the jury returned a verdict of 'not guilty' and he was discharged.

INDECENT ASSAULT, GATESHEAD, 1874

William Robinson, a rather dirty and dishevelled-looking individual, was charged at Gateshead Police Court on 16 March with having indecently assaulted Ann Chambers in a railway carriage. Mr Campbell, railway superintendent, conducted the case for the prosecution. He said that the defendant, who had been employed at Tyne Dock as a temporary trimmer, had taken the 1.40 train from Newcastle to Malton. On 26 February Miss Chambers had entered the same compartment at Gateshead. Seeing that he was about to start smoking, she pointed out politely that they were in a non-smoking compartment. He then proceeded to tell her that he liked her appearance and asked her to shake hands with him, but she indignantly refused. As the train was passing through the tunnel near Redheugh, he seized hold of her with his left hand, and attacked her with his right. She screamed out, and as the train emerged from the tunnel, 'he was seen rising'.

Other passengers gave evidence to confirm the assault. Robinson was found guilty and sentenced to three months' imprisonment.

Gateshead Policemen, c. 1880 (Photograph courtesy of the Libraries & Arts Service, Gateshead Council)

ATTEMPTED SUICIDE, WEST AUCKLAND, 1875

On the night of Sunday 3 January John Palmer, a farrier, made a determined attempt to take his own life at his lodgings in New Street, West Auckland. Having been depressed for a long time, at about 7.00 p.m. he went into the back kitchen and tried to cut his throat with a pocketknife. His landlady immediately sent for Dr Richardson and Sergeant Cruikshank. His windpipe was severed, but the jugular vein was unharmed and he was expected to make a full recovery.

While being apprehended by the police, he lashed out and struggled so violently that the sergeant had to use handcuffs on him and keep guard on him all night.

ASSAULT AND DAMAGE, STOCKTON, 1875

At Stockton Police Court on 4 January 1875, John Young was charged with assaulting Dorothy Tyson, landlady of the Commercial Inn, Norton, and with wilful damage to the door of the house. He had gone to the inn at about 10.30 on the evening of Saturday 2 January for a drink, but she refused to serve him as he was already quite drunk. Not content to go quietly, he made a scene and lashed out at several of the patrons, then struck Mrs Tyson. After being sent off the premises he smashed a window and broke open a door.

For the breakages he was fined 1s damages, 1s 6d and 4s 6d costs, or seven days, and for the assault he was fined 10s and 5s 10d costs, or fourteen days, with one sentence to follow the other.

ATTEMPTED MURDER, STOCKTON, 1875

On 25 April 1875 forty-two-year-old Thomas Dublin was at Mr Larkin's lodging house in Shoulder of Mutton Yard at Stockton. That night he, labourer Timothy Madden and Richard Parkinson were in an upstairs room — the bedroom where Madden and Dublin slept — in the house until just before midnight. There was a dispute between Parkinson and Dublin, with the latter accusing the former of being 'a bully in the house'. At this Parkinson jumped up, struck Dublin, knocked him over and jumped on him a couple of times. Dublin then got up, and went downstairs, saying he was going to fetch the police. Parkinson followed soon afterwards, and Mrs Parkinson called out in horror that Dublin had stabbed her husband with a knife.

Madden immediately got dressed, went downstairs, and found Mr and Mrs Parkinson in the kitchen. Parkinson was sitting on a chair, holding his hand to his side, evidently in pain, as he confirmed his wife's statement. A little while later he collapsed. A doctor was called, and on examination found that Parkinson's bowels were protruding. Dublin was arrested and next day he was taken before the Stockton Borough Magistrates, charged with stabbing and with intent to kill.

He went on trial on 13 July at Durham Assizes, where the evidence suggested that Dublin had made preparations with a knife to stab Parkinson. It was fortunate that the latter had recovered from not very serious injuries, as if he had died, Dublin would have probably faced execution on a capital charge. He was sentenced to seven years' penal servitude.

Murderous attack, Thornley, 1875

John Young, of the Durham County Constabulary, was on duty at Thornley on the night of 4 December 1875 when he came across a man attacking a woman. He seized the man by the collar, and the woman ran off. Soon afterwards five men, including Roger Halliday, and John and Robert Robinson, all pitmen, set upon Young and attacked him with a heavy stick. Having knocked him over, they kicked him all over the body and in the head. He shouted for help and Constable Frost, accompanied by Mr Clark, came to the rescue, whereupon the men ran away. Frost and Clark found Halliday and Robert Robinson hiding behind some railway wagons, their hands and boots stained with blood. A bruised and still bleeding Young was escorted home. He remained off work for six weeks, and for some time after that he was still feeling dizzy each morning.

At Durham Spring Assizes on 1 March 1876 Young admitted that in the past he had been fined for drunkenness, but he was sober on the night of the incident in question. Two witnesses for the defence said that he was nevertheless under the influence of alcohol at the time, one claiming he was so drunk he could not walk. Dr William Nesbitt, who had examined him after the attack, said he had three scalp wounds, and his head was so badly bruised that he was in considerable danger for some time. John Robinson was discharged, but the other two were found guilty of unlawful wounding.

Mr Justice Mellor sentenced them to fifteen months' hard labour, saying that he would be failing in his duty if he did not pass upon them a serious sentence for assaulting a constable in the execution of his duty.

Serving Drunken Customer, Witton Gilbert, 1877

At Durham County Police Court on 4 July 1877 William Barker, landlord of the Glendenning Arms at Witton Gilbert, was charged with serving a drunken customer on 19 July. That day Thomas Seymour, a mason, staggered into the inn and asked for two glasses of whisky, one for himself and one for Barker. Mrs Seymour followed her husband in and suggested he should not serve him, as he was so drunk. Disregarding her advice, Barker supplied the glasses of whisky, and took the money for them as he said he was prepared to supply his customer drink as long as he could pay for it. In her presence he also served another drunken man with beer, and when Mrs Barker objected, he threatened to 'kick her out' if she did not go away and leave him alone.

He told the bench that it had not been beer but ginger beer, but the bench considered the case was proved. Mr Barker had already had one similar conviction, and this time he was fined £5 plus costs, as well as an order being made for his licence to be endorsed with the conviction.

BURGLARY, COXHOE, 1877

At Durham County Police Court on 4 July, Mrs Margaret Gardner was charged with 'burglariously entering' the Collier Inn, Coxhoe, on 29 June. William Atkinson and his wife, the licensees, were woken about midnight by a noise in the cellar. He got up to open the door, and there was a strong smell of rum. As neither of them dared to go downstairs, he opened the window and shouted 'Police!' Assistance came, and they made a search of the premises. Mrs Gardner was found in the cellar, and the tap of a keg of rum was running to waste on the ground beside her. Thoroughly drunk, she was given into police custody, while an examination of the premises showed that she had obtained access through a small window. She had sawed away the trellised woodwork to gain admittance, and she was very wet, having fallen into a well. Five gallons of rum were missing, each valued at 18s 6d, or in total £4 12s 6d, as well as a bottle of brandy and other goods.

Mrs Gardner explained that she had gone into the cellar to hide from her husband, who was ill-using her. Rum was missing from two kegs, and it was assumed to have been passed to somebody outside. In the absence of further evidence, the bench reduced the charge to one of being found on premises for an unlawful purpose, and sentenced the defendant to one month's imprisonment with hard labour.

MANSLAUGHTER, SUNDERLAND, 1878

On 9 February 1878, a husband and wife argument broke out in Dignan's lodging house at Low Street in Sunderland. At about 1.30 p.m. Catherine Burns came into the kitchen where some other lodgers were present. She picked up a poker, walked over to the fireplace, stirred the fire with it and laid it down. She was followed by her husband John, and almost at once they began arguing. Tempers flared, and he picked the poker up. Thrusting it in her direction, the point caught her in the throat, and she fell forward. In a panic he tried to stop the blood from flowing. However, the wound had gone too deep, and it was to no avail. He took her upstairs and laid her on the bed, but within half an hour she was dead.

John Burns attacking his wife (Illustrated Police News)

The case obviously fell short of murder, but he was arrested and appeared at Durham Assizes on 22 March before Mr Baron Pollock. Mr Ridley prosecuted, and nobody appeared for the defence. Nevertheless a penitent Burns was able to argue convincingly that it had been a terrible accident, and that he had been provoked. The jury found him guilty of manslaughter, but added a recommendation to mercy. He was sentenced to six months' hard labour.

MANSLAUGHTER, GATESHEAD, 1879

On 11 October 1879 John Keeney, aged about twenty-five, a labourer from Gateshead, had a quarrel with his stepmother Eliza, aged about fifty. She and her second husband Michael, also a labourer, lived at Leonard's Court, and John had been living with them for several weeks. While they were standing at the top of the stairs an argument began, and he told her that if she did not go downstairs he would push her. She refused, he took hold of her by the shoulders and she fell backwards down thirteen steps. The neighbours heard a noise, came indoors to see what was happening, and picked her up, but she was unconscious. A doctor was called, but she remained in a coma for the next seven days, suffered a brain haemorrhage, and died at about 10.30 p.m. on 18 October.

Keeney was remanded and charged with manslaughter at Durham Assizes before Mr Justice Bower on 31 October, but he pleaded 'not guilty', as he declared he had never intended to push her. He was found 'not guilty' and acquitted.

BIBLIOGRAPHY

Appleton, Arthur, *Mary Ann Cotton, Her Story and Trial*, Michael Joseph, 1973

Emsley, John, *The Elements of Murder: A History of Poison*, OUP, 2005

Fielding, Steve, *Hanged at Durham*, History Press, 2008

Fielding, Steve, *The Hangman's Record*, Vol. 1, 1868-1899; Vol. 2, 1900-1929; Vol. 3, 1930-1964, CBD, 1994-2005

Green, Nigel, *Tough Times and Grisly Crimes: A History of Crime in Northumberland and County Durham*, the Author, 2005

Jones, Steve, *Northumberland and Durham: The Sinister Side*, Wicked, 1999

Ramsland, Katherine M., *Inside the Minds of Serial Killers*, Greenwood, 2006

Watson, Katherine, *Poisoned Lives*, Hambledon, 2003

Whitehead, Tony, *Mary Ann Cotton, Dead but Not Forgotten*, the Author, 2000

Oxford Dictionary of National Biography

Newspapers

Aberdeen Journal

Birmingham Daily Post

Bristol Mercury

Derby Mercury

Glasgow Herald

The Graphic

Leeds Mercury

Liverpool Mercury

Lloyds Weekly

Manchester News

Newcastle Courant

Northern Echo

The Times

Western Mail